Dark Psychology and Manipulation

Martin McGray

Table of Contents

Introduction

Before you begin to learn about the different methods of dark psychology and know how to use them or defend yourself against them, I want you to know what this type of control is all about, how the human mind works, and how it is sustained throughout our lives. The truth is that we see this type of psychology everywhere, in advertising, in the bosses, and we have even used it without being aware that we do it.

Knowing well what it is about is not a simple mission, so many people cannot do it. Learning the different principles of psychology is not necessary; you just have to start implementing the various techniques that I will be showing you and clear the concepts. Only with the book that you have on your hands can you begin to do your first manipulations, and you will achieve a solid base. You will have the power to understand people, know what motivates them, and figure out why they may react in different ways. In addition to this, you can spend time taking classes and reading many books to get a complete understanding; it depends on how far you want to go with this. So, if only a few people understand what this type of psychology is, why is it so important that you know how to use and interpret it? It is because those who know what it is and how to use it can apply this power either for their benefit or to defend themselves.

Dark psychology is any type of behavior that can be questionable or even criminal; it depends on who uses it. It can even affect innocent people. The one who uses this psychology takes advantage of who he considers weak or who has vulnerabilities. This means that they are not weak as such, but they are easily influenced or read for the benefit of the manipulator.

Dark psychology is present in the world. The manipulator will always find vulnerabilities in others to benefit themselves; they will use lies, love dependency, manipulations, persuasion, and anything else to get what they want. He usually succeeds because he can easily read the person he is trying to attack.

Many people who live in denial assume that dark psychology is not there and that it is not a problem they have to deal with; they think that this type of psychology is not even bad. Others may choose to remain ignorant about it, or they may learn to take control and protect themselves and even others from manipulations.

Being able to understand this is not just to defend oneself. Many principles and ideas are within the world of dark psychology, and only by knowing them, you will be able to be aware of the person using the techniques. They are a series of knowledge that will be useful to you every time a person tries to use the techniques against you or when you want to use them to achieve some goal on your own. When you pull back the curtain on the world of psychology, you will realize that there is more to human nature than you ever imagined. We will see in this book how this can work.

Although some people may use this information to achieve wrong actions, many will use it for good purposes, for example, to gain promotion, but without harming others, and there will be many who will use it as a mode of defense.

Some of these tools have been learned involuntarily by people due to the situations and experiences they have had to live through. Let's talk hypothetically: when you were a child, you saw how adults behaved, especially those closest to you. Or when you were a teenager, and your ability to understand the behaviors around you expanded, you could see others with their tactics and then how they succeeded. Later you used these techniques unintentionally at first, but when you discovered that you did well, you began to use them intentionally. There are people like politicians who use them, public speakers, or technology salesman who wants to offer the new and best hardware or software in the world, as he sees it.

You will learn many tactics in this book that you can regularly use, hopefully with good intentions.

You can, for example, give someone love, congratulate or praise people for accomplishing something you want them to do, help them with something in the office, whatever. You just have to lavish them with love to make them feel good, and this might make them more likely to help you.

If you are a great manipulator, you could make them feel attached to you and ask them to do things they usually don't do.

You can use tools such as lying or telling a person a false version of the situation; you can also manipulate them with partial truths or get them to do what you want.

Denial is another form of manipulation. This can be hard on the other person because it can make them feel lost and abandoned by what you do. This is accomplished by withholding affection and love until you get what you want from that person.

Among the many tools I will show you in this book, there is also withdrawal, which is when the person is given the silent treatment, or you avoid them until they do what you want.

There is also a choice restriction, which is when the manipulator gives the victim access to some choices but does so to distract them from others they don't want them to consider. Finally, there is also semantic manipulation, which is a strategy where you use words commonly known to both parties in a conversation but then you tell the other person that they had a different meaning and this new meaning will change their perception completely; you can do this so that the conversation goes the way you want, thus fooling the other person.

Who can use these dark tools? Anyone who wants to. However, keep in mind that many people can also use them against you. They can be found at many points in your life, so you must learn to stay away from them; some people can use dark psychology to harm you.

If you go to the literature on dark psychology, you will find that narcissists are part of those who would use it because these kinds of people have an exaggerated sense of their self-worth, and they need others to see them as superior. They may use dark psychology to fulfill their desire to be worshipped as gods.

It can also be intuited that sociopaths, who are charming, intelligent, and persuasive, would use this tool to do whatever they want. They are generally emotionless and do not feel remorse. This means that they have no problem with using these tactics; they get what they want at any price. They can even create superficial relationships.

The others are politicians, who, with the help of dark psychology, can convince people to vote for them simply by persuading citizens that what they offer is the best and that they have the absolute truth.

Although a seller can do it too, not all of them do it, but the good ones, the ones with the sharp verb, surely do it. Those who suddenly want to sell you the latest technology gadget will use it to increase their sales and tell you anything with their tools; this way, you will buy something convinced that you are getting the best and maybe it is not so.

Leaders also know how to use this tool; they use it so that the other subordinates, and all those who listen to them, obey them. In the literature, you will also find that selfish people use these tools and make sure that their needs are put first before the rest; they do not care about anyone and even make others give up their benefits so that they profit. If it doesn't serve them, then it may serve someone else of their choice.

The list of what you will read in this book is long, and it will serve you to protect yourself and use it for good. You will be able to manipulate and protect yourself from manipulation. One of the goals of this book is to help you be aware of those who want to get something out of you without worrying about how it will affect you. We also pretend to arm you well with dark psychology principles.

Another topic I will cover in the book is persuasion, which is a fascinating subject. Society considers many types of persuasion as good. They accept them and even have jobs where they spend a lot of time persuading other people. Any attempt on the part of one person to influence the other can already be considered a form of persuasion.

An example is the computer salesman who tries to persuade another to buy the newest and best graphics card, which also has an incredible price. This is not seen as evil or sinister; the difference is that this persuasion and other examples like this benefit both parties, the one who buys the graphics card and the seller who has his profit.

Many legitimate types of persuasion are not considered dark psychology, and the computer salesman is one of them. The same can be said of negotiators who use their skills to persuade a terrorist to release the hostages. If a person is persuaded to go to an event they are going to enjoy, then it is a good way to convince; it can be taken as positive persuasion. So, what is dark persuasion?

To understand which is positive and which is negative, it is good to know what is behind each one, that is, the intentions. Positive persuasion is used to encourage someone to do something without getting hurt, for example, when the negotiator succeeds in rescuing hostages who are in danger, then it serves to save lives.

With dark persuasion, there is no moral motive; the motive can be amoral and often immoral. If positive persuasion is understood as a way to help others, then dark persuasion is a process to get people to act against what they want to do. Sometimes people will do things reluctantly, knowing that they are likely to make a bad decision, but they do so because they are anxious to stop persuasion efforts. In other cases, the persuader will make the victim think they acted wisely, but in this case, the victim does the opposite.

What are the intentions of a person using dark persuasion? This depends on the situation and the individual who is using it. For example, some people like to persuade others to cause physical or mental harm; others use it to benefit themselves, or because they delight in the pain they cause to people.

Some enjoy the control of this type of persuasion, and some want to achieve results with this manipulation.

One of these scenarios is achieved with positive persuasion, but the benefit always goes to the person persuaded. There is a win-win benefit for the persuader and the persuaded; there is a mutual benefit for the convinced person and the other. All of these results are good because they involve a positive outcome for the person persuaded. Sometimes there will be those who benefit from the actions. But in all 3 situations, the persuaded party always benefits.

With dark persuasion, the result is different: the one who persuades is the one who always benefits when he exercises control. The one who is influenced usually goes against his self-interest and does not benefit from this type of persuasion.

Those who persuade are skillful: they cause harm to others and benefit themselves and can also harm in the process. Much can be accomplished by removing the mask from the one who persuades with dark intentions.

Surely, you want to know who around you might be using this type of persuasion; their characteristics are that they are indifferent or cannot care about how the influence will affect others. They are people who use this kind of persuasion and behave like narcissists, considering their needs as more important than those of others. They may even be sociopaths and cannot understand other people's feelings.

On many occasions, this kind of dark persuasion appears in relationships. But sometimes, friends are also inclined to use dark persuasion against each other. If the attempts are persistent and long-lasting, then this relationship is classified as psychologically abusive and is not healthy for the victim.

Sometimes they do not realize that something is going on or that they are being persuaded, and by the time they realize it is too late and they are stuck there. I will share with you many cases and tools in this book. One would be, for example, if a partner does not allow you to open a business in your area, and, at the same time, does everything to convince you that it is not the best thing to do; he might even act selfishly to convince you of what he wants.

In the following pages, you will learn about manipulation, persuasion, and all that is dark psychology, either to use it or not to let others use it on you.

Chapter 1: What Is Dark Persuasion and Dark Psychology?

First of all, I want you to know the different tools that exist to manipulate, persuade, and control people, which are part of dark psychology. Learning these concepts is essential so that we can then go into how they influence your life, how you can use them if that is your objective, or how they can use them on you.

Dark psychology has been widely treated by many authors; some have contradicted themselves, but, in essence, it is how a person acts with gestures or actions to manipulate you and get what they want from you. I describe below the different meanings with examples.

Dark Persuasion, What Is It?

In the introduction, I already gave you a brief description of it, but I will remind you once again. It is when, with tools and actions, you prepare a person to accept a point of view or do something you want according to your intentions or the intentions of the other.

When you use it, you may not respect the other person's feelings and beliefs, and what you do is motivate the relationship of the other person's wants or needs. You set it in motion to achieve a win-win result for both of you or simply for you, who has the intention and the goal.

It can be used by giving the necessary information so that the other person chooses what is best for them according to their interests, by stating what they have to lose and what they have to gain in return. The final results are effective and with great permanence, achieving a convincing effect.

I will explain this concept in more detail so that you can understand it.

Dark Persuasion Principles

To make good use of the following basic principles, you must remember that persuasion is not the same as manipulation. Manipulation means imposing coercion to force the behavior of others for the sake of one party. The power of persuasion must be accompanied by flexible behavior, the ability to transfer energy and remain calm in conflict situations, as well as effective communication and, of course, adequate professional preparation.

Everyone can be persuaded at the right time and in the right context, although not necessarily in a short term. That is why political movements are focusing their time and money in particular on groups of undecided voters. The first step in persuasion is to identify those who are interested in your point of view at a specific time and focus your energy on them. When someone wants to sell a technology to a person, the salesperson who wants to persuade does so with the undecided because it puts the seeds of doubt in their minds, supposedly by appeasing them.

Context and timing are the basic components of persuasion. The former creates a standard around acceptable behavior, while the latter dictates what to expect from others and life.

You cannot persuade someone who is not interested in what you have to say. The first art of persuasion is learning to keep talking to people about themselves, and if you do, you will get their full attention.

The necessary reciprocity is when someone does something for you, and you feel obligated to do something for that person. Helping each other is an action that helps us survive as a species; it is part of our evolutionary

DNA. By offering small gestures of caring to others, you can ask for more in return.

People who are willing to follow through on their claims, desires, and goals without losing courage are ultimately the most compelling. Several historical figures have been persistent in their efforts and message. Abraham Lincoln lost his mother, 3 sons, a sister, and his girlfriend; he also failed in business and lost 8 elections before being elected president of the United States.

Another way to persuade is to use congratulations. Compliments have a positive impact on people, and with this, they may begin to trust because you make them feel good. There are many reasons to congratulate someone; do it sincerely (or at least make it seem that way).

You can also set expectations. Persuasion is also about managing the expectations of others. For example, a CEO who promises a 20% increase in sales and achieves a 30% increase is rewarded. In other words, exceeding the expectations of those around you will improve your persuasion ability.

Don't assume that others always receive value, don't assume that they need something. Don't take for granted what others want or don't want; offer what can be offered.

The other thing is that you can create a sense of urgency. You have to be able to instill a sense of urgency where people want to take immediate action. If they're not motivated enough to want something right now, they're less likely to find motivation in the future. Try to convince people that immediate action is needed.

The other is, to tell the truth, or a lie but to say it with such firmness that it seems to be true. Sometimes, the most effective way to convince people is to tell them what they don't want to say. Over time, putting the last word on the table will increase your persuasion.

Dark Psychology, What Is It?

Now, I will talk about dark psychology, showing you how dark it is; I will speak about Machiavellianism, manipulation, and psychopathy.

Machiavellianism comes from Nicolas Machiavelli, who lived in the 1500s. He wrote a treatise on a political doctrine called *"The Prince."* Everyone on this planet has heard the phrase, "The end justifies the means," which was not said by Machiavelli, although it is attributed to him. What happened is that he was summoned to work as a negotiator. He was a great negotiator who, based on his vast experience, managed to write a treatise where he could define different ways to come to power, in his case, how to become a prince. Today, he is an example of how to become a politician or have power in something.

There we go to manipulation, which has several meanings: One of which is intervening with skillful means to achieve a benefit. The other is to control subtly by preventing the opinions of the rest from developing. When we talk about manipulation, something to keep in mind is that the manipulator uses the victim as a tool, nothing like Machiavelli's subtlety; in this case, they are tools for their purpose.

I must clarify something else: there is no manipulator without the victim. On the other hand, what must be taken into account when talking about manipulation is the fact of exercising power. There are several forms: one is the power to punish, the power to inform, and the power of reputation. All of this is considered as the image that the manipulator creates in the victim: that he (or she) is someone important, imposing, and that they cannot be questioned. This generates in the target the feeling of not being able to do or say anything. When they cannot, they create a bigger image than the manipulator has.

We also have psychopathy. It can be defined as a lack of empathy, but it does not necessarily imply that those who suffer from this disease are murderers. The psychopath is not only the one who kills; not all of them do it. In psychopathy, I will summarize some aspects to take into account to determine when psychopaths are around.

Just as with manipulation, the psychopath uses people as objects to achieve his or her goals. One of the issues they have is that they suddenly treat you aggressively, and then, as if nothing happened, they talk to you normally. However, someone who does that doesn't necessarily have to be a psychopath.

Another issue is manipulation. Sometimes, the person that is manipulated is not aware of it, and then, when they learn the message, they may realize it. Other times, the manipulated person does not realize that they are being lied to. Another common feature is that psychopaths seem to enjoy the damage they cause to people.

Dark psychology is the art and science of manipulation and control. While psychology is the study of human behavior and the core of our thoughts, actions, and interactions, the term dark psychology is the phenomenon by which people use strategies of motivation, persuasion, manipulation, and coercion to get what they want.

Those who study psychology, depending on which branch they work on, may be familiar with the term "dark triad," which refers to what many criminologists and psychologists point to as simple predictors of criminal behavior, as well as of couple breakups and problematic relationships.

I'll explain what the Dark Triad is all about, although I'll expand on the topic later in detail:

Narcissism

It is selfishness, grandiosity, and lack of empathy.

Machiavellianism

I explained it before. It tries to use manipulation to deceive and exploit people. They may not even have a sense of morality in their actions.

Psychopathy

He is usually charming and friendly but is characterized by impulsivity, selfishness, lack of empathy, and lack of self-blame.

None of us wants to be the victim of manipulation, but it happens all the time.

We may not be particularly in touch with someone who is part of the dark triad, but ordinary people like you, and like most of us, deal with dark psychological strategies daily.

Manipulation Tactics in Dark Psychology

These tactics are often found in commercials, online ads, sales techniques, and even in your boss's actions. If you have children (especially teenagers), you surely experience these strategies when they experiment with certain behaviors to get what they want while seeking autonomy.

Indeed, people, you trust and love often use covert manipulation and dark persuasion.

These are some of the tactics most commonly used by ordinary people:

- **Love flooding:** The affection, the overwhelming of a person so that they will do what you want.

- **Lying:** Exaggerating, telling false things, half-truths, or unrealistic stories.

- **Denial of love:** Used to deprive the individual of attention and affection.

- **Abstinence:** You try to avoid the person or refuse to talk to them.

- **Choice restriction:** Given some choice options that distract from the choice you don't want a person to make.

- **Reverse psychology:** You tell the person one thing or do something to motivate them to do the opposite, what you truly want.

- **Semantic manipulation:** You use words that are supposed to have a common or mutual definition, but the manipulator will tell you that they have a different definition and understanding of the conversation. Words are powerful and important.

While some people who use these tactics know exactly what they are doing and intend to manipulate you to get what they want, others use underhanded and unethical actions without fully realizing it.

Many of these people learned these strategies from their parents during childhood. Others learned these strategies by accident when they were teenagers or adults. They unknowingly used manipulation tactics, and it worked for them; they got what they wanted. Therefore, they continue using the strategies that helped them succeed.

In some cases, people are trained to use these strategies. Training programs that teach unethical and obscure psychology and persuasion strategies are often sales or marketing programs.

Many of these programs use underhanded tactics to build brands or sell products whose sole purpose is to serve themselves or their company, not their customers. Many of these training programs convince people that using these strategies is okay and beneficial to buyers. Because, of course, their lives are much better when they buy a product or service.

According to Psychology and Studies, Which People Use Dark Psychology and Manipulation?

Here is a list of those who seem to usually use these strategies:

- **Narcissist:** A genuinely narcissistic person (fits the clinical diagnosis) has an inflated sense of self-worth. They need others to validate their belief in their superiority. They dream of being adored and praised. They use dark psychological tactics, manipulation, and unethical persuasion to sustain themselves.
- **Sociopath:** A true sociopath (a clinical diagnosis) is often charming, intelligent, but impulsive. Lacking emotions and blaming themselves, they use dark tactics to build superficial relationships and then take advantage of people.
- **Lawyers:** There may be lawyers who focus on winning the case and use dark persuasion tactics to get what they want.
- **Politicians:** some politicians use these psychological and dark persuasion tactics to convince others that they are right to get votes.

- **Salespeople:** Some salespeople are so focused on making sales that they use dark tools to motivate and persuade someone to buy the product.
- **Leaders:** Some leaders use these tactics to get things done they want or get others to perform better.
- **Public speakers:** Some speakers use sleazy tactics to increase the emotional state of their audience, knowing that it will generate more product sales in the back of the room.
- **Selfish people:** They can be anyone who has an agenda ahead of others. They will use strategies to satisfy their own needs first, even at the expense of others. They don't care about winning or losing. In this case, it could be a man who wants to become a technology project manager and manipulates anyone to get that coveted promotion even though others deserve that position before him.

Ethical vs. Shady Practices

It is important to evaluate your intentions to differentiate between arcane and persuasive motivational strategies from ethical ones. You have to ask yourself if your strategies are designed to help others. The intention to help you is also good, but you can easily fall into shady and unethical practices if it is only for your benefit.

Achieving mutually beneficial, win-win results should be the goal. However, you must be honest with yourself and trust that the other person will benefit.

An example of this is an app marketer who believes that everyone will benefit from their product and that their download will improve customers' lives. With this mindset, marketers can easily use sleazy tactics to push people to buy and use a "purpose is good" mentality. This allows people to adopt any strategies to get sales. But the truth is that all of a sudden, that application is somewhere else and, by the way, for free.

Dark Psychology Principles

Deeply studied in applied and clinical psychology are the dark triads. More recently, this has also been considered by corporate management.

Well, dark triads are those who score high on assessments, indicating that they have the potential to cause discomfort and problems, which would be a struggle if they were to assume higher leadership positions.

People who score high on these assessment tests may experience discomfort in the work environment because they are less empathetic, sympathetic, compassionate, disagreeable, etc.

In short, the term dark triad is addressed in the field of psychology, including those characteristics of narcissistic, psychotic, or Machiavellian personality traits.

It was named "Dark" because its qualities included a touch of malice or insensitivity in expressing emotions, as well as aggressive behavior and a tendency to be insincere or untruthful.

From an evolutionary perspective, the origins of clinical research in psychiatry first appeared in 1941 in The Mask of Sanity by H. Cleckley. The first people to start talking about this triad were authors Delroy L. Paulhus and Kevin M. William in 2002. Another study is that of psychologist Fernando Moraga entitled The Dark Triad of Personality: Machiavellianism, Narcissism, and Psychopathy, published in 2015.

But, in 1991, it was Robert Hale who made this triad more widely studied and known to more people, thanks to his book The Psychiatric Checklist-Revised (PCL-R)."

Although Hale's book focuses on issues already behind bars, it is known to go a step further today.

Let's look at the traits of psychopathy, which are part of these principles, based on those that Cleckey proposed in 1976 as traits that could be defined as subclinical psychopathy, which are:

- A great superficial charm that is appealing from the start.
- An outstanding intelligence.
- Lack of irrational thoughts.
- Absence of hallucinations.
- Do not show any kind of nervousness.
- Lack of sincerity or falsehood.
- Antisocial behaviors cannot be justified.
- No capacity to feel shame.
- Not able to feel remorse.
- Has trouble learning from experiences.
- Not able to love.
- Egocentrism.
- Loss of intuition.
- Little affection.
- Insensitivity.
- Exaggerated behaviors, whether under the influence of alcohol or not.
- Suicide threats are rarely carried out.
- Poor ability to make a life plan or to follow it.
- A frivolous sexual life.
- Unstable emotional relationships.

All these details are revealed when the word dark psychology is mentioned. As I was saying, they acquire relevance nowadays because, in various environments, it is considered very important to make a psychological approach to people to filter out all those who are believed to have these characteristics: those who cheat in exams, those who have dishonest behaviors to climb positions, those who create conflicts in the environment, etc.

Is Dark Persuasion Bad?

I think that was clearer to you in the previous paragraphs, and the truth is not that it is bad. As long as you use it to convince someone to do something, but in the end, they end up winning.

Suppose you persuade someone to give up their intention to get a promotion because you will use it to your benefit and tell them that you are a better option. In that case, you are undoubtedly a bad person who uses dark persuasion for an immoral purpose.

Now, if you are a Big Data specialist and you convince that businessman that taking the step with you is going to help him to have his systems more secure and that, although your costs are high, the guarantee of a good price is written, then that businessman wins, and you win because you have a new client and a juicy salary. Here dark persuasion was fine because you used it to make everyone win.

But suppose you sell a no-good app. In that case, that is about a cryptocurrency game where they convince people that it's the deal of the century where everyone will earn a lot of coins just for signing up and playing, buying their first tokens, but you know it's not going to work. You're sure to use it for dark purposes.

In short, you are the one who decides if you use it for good or bad purposes.

Is Dark Psychology Bad?

According to the above, it depends on the purposes you give it; it will always depend on how you want to achieve your goals. When you use psychology with bad intentions, you harm people, hurt them, and cause them damage that they do not even realize in many cases. But when you use it to manipulate a politician or leader to give resources to help improve your community, maybe asphalt the streets or better the street lighting, then you are using it with good intentions.

What Positive Uses Can Be Made of Persuasion and Dark Psychology?

In the world in which we live and work, persuasion is an essential skill for almost all of us. This is a key aspect not only professionally but also personally. For example, it is helpful in everyday situations, such as trying to convince your partner to go to the movies or take your children to a specific school, and in work situations, such as convincing company directors to accept a cybersecurity reform. We need to market our ideas and opinions, products, services... Even our talents and reputation. Persuasion is an aspect that touches every area of our lives and is not only part of public discourse but also plays a crucial role in interpersonal communication.

Persuasion is the art of leading to the adoption of ideas, attitudes, or actions that people believe will benefit them in one way or another. It is trying to win others over in discussions: it is not about beating them; it is about getting to where the other is.

Persuasion is interactive and tries to meet the needs of both parties. It is, therefore, a 2-way process with 2 directions. It is about people who want to persuade, using reason, credibility, and emotional appeal, to lead their audience to embrace a belief, value, attitude, or behavior freely.

I will show you these three situations in which persuasion skills are crucial:

1. Changing People's Attitudes, Opinions, and Behaviors

If people are unhappy with a situation, it is easy to invite them to change because we are satisfying their conscious or unconscious desire for something new. However, if they are comfortable with their beliefs and how they do things, they will resist any change because they will insist that there is no real need for it. If I'm not interested, why should I change? This is a complex issue. Persuasion seeks only voluntary change (without deceptive promises, coercion, or manipulation).

2. Improving Beliefs, Attitudes, and Behaviors

When people are optimistic about what we tell them, we just need to reinforce it. As speakers, we should remind our audience that they freely choose this attitude and try to reinforce it. For example, a clergyman at Sunday Mass often reaches audiences who are convinced that they will strengthen their faith by hearing the Catholic Mass. Such audiences need to be motivated.

3. Building Attitudes and Opinions

The best example is the teacher and their students. Teachers try to shape students' responses positively. Generally, if students respect their knowledge and position, teachers will not have reliability problems.

The ability to persuade involves identifying what people care about, finding common ground (including values), structuring our arguments to emphasize what is in their favor, and placing this information in the right emotional context.

As for using dark psychology to your advantage without hurting anyone, **here are some tools you can use as long as you don't end up hurting that person:**

- If you smile at the person to influence them. You transmit happiness, but it is something you might do to get someone to let you pass even though they have already closed a place, or you smile at the obnoxious official who prevented you from passing to stamp a document. That smile on your face makes them more willing to accept what you are asking for.

- You can take advantage of a person's tiredness to get what you want without hurting the person. Maybe you try to convince someone to accept a project, and you take advantage of it when they are exhausted. This is something that cults know well. That's why brainwashing sessions, which I'll get to later, use long and exhausting sessions to convince you of something. They know that a tired person has low defenses and accepts or obeys what they say.

- The other thing is sucking up. Ego is one of the weak points of people; we all want to hear good things, and we have the disposition to attend to a person who makes us feel good. It is not easy to flatter without being noticed. If you suck up, you have to use your intelligence, for example, you like the girl in systems, but she hasn't said "yes" yet, so sucking up can help convince her to go out with you.

- Another technique is to make her say "yes" many times to that person. If you want to cause influence, make her say "yes" in the conversation several times. When she says "yes" many times, the brain understands that she is in tune with the person she is talking to, and the inertia of answering "yes" can be good for her to respond affirmatively.

It is widely used in commercials and those who want to sell something:

- Do you want the best cybersecurity on your systems? Yes.
- Do you like to save on systems costs? Yes.
- Do you like everything to work properly? Yes.
- Do you want to listen to a special offer I have for you? Yes.

Sucking up and saying "yes" a lot of times are a couple of effective techniques and can be used with good intentions.

Although these good intentions are a topic I will touch on in the next chapter, I hope that the knowledge you will see will be used in your favor and not to harm others.

Chapter 2: Using Persuasion to Your Advantage

You already know the basics of persuasion and dark psychology and that it can be used with both good and bad intentions. Now, I want you to learn how to use it to your advantage, and you will decide the intentions.

Persuasion can be used to help you connect with other people. I'm not saying use it with bad intentions to do your bidding and hurt someone. There are many ways to put it to work with good intentions. That's what I'll talk about in this chapter: how you can connect with others, whether it's to seduce a person you like, get a promotion, or if you're looking for a job and want them to give the job to you.

Using persuasion to your advantage is an essential requirement to develop and progress, of course, as long as you use it with good intentions.

Persuading to Achieve a Romantic Relationship

Now, I want to show you how to persuade to achieve a romantic relationship with whoever you want, but before you do it, you have to follow a series of guidelines:

Plan Everything to the Millimeter

If you feel you are not fully prepared, you will fail. Think about how you want the conversation to go: where and how. Maybe in the office, where there is enough noise, or where, on the contrary, there is much silence, and he or she can hear you. Think about all those little details.

Think about that person's possible objections and be prepared to broach the subject. Start by saying, "Maybe you'll tell me you don't want to go out this Friday because you have to take care of your son, but how about if I help you get him a lullaby, and you and I go out to dinner?"

Be Clear About What You Want and Why

Maybe you want to go out with that woman because you have liked her for a long time and you feel that she is the one with whom you want to live the sunset of your life, have a new youth, or go for a walk in a country.

Or, on the contrary, you are very attracted to her, and you want to have a fun time with her, have a good time, sex, but without committing yourself. You must be clear about what you want and why you are taking this step.

Be Certain of the Type of Person You Want to Convince

Some people approach debates and exchanges as if their goal is simply for the truth to triumph over lies. That is, they set a goal in the abstract in which the real message, because it is real, always ends up convincing everyone who hears it. However, if what you want is not just to be morally superior to someone, but to be truly convincing, then this is a big mistake.

For example, exposing the incoherence in the other person's mouth, drawing attention to the fact that he or she does not admit to correcting, can be interpreted as a symptom that they do not understand what they are talking about. On the other hand, if you are trying to convince that person, this strategy is incorrect because, as a result, he or she takes a more defensive attitude, making it difficult for them to change their mind due to cognitive dissonance. We will talk about this next.

Attracting or seducing with persuasion is a job you have to do consciously; you have to be awake and attentive to the message you want to convey and the physical and verbal responses you receive from the person you want to seduce. One way to achieve this is to design your phrases to attract.

Remember, everyone is different; so, be creative. When it comes to attraction and engagement, the only point that truly matters is having a conversation that makes people feel comfortable and relaxed. Therefore, phrases to seduce or fascinate should connect with the imaginary realm, thus creating an intimate emotional bond with others.

Phrases such as "don't you think that..." "Imagine what would happen if..." Can help you strengthen your ability to captivate, as positive phrases allow you to create positive emotional bonds.

Use positive language: Sometimes, the people around you or yourself are often negative, so try changing the "no" to provide a confident affirmation. To attract and seduce, speak positively, and make the other person feel safe.

Stay in control: Don't run out of conversation topics in the first meeting. To attract or seduce, it is more important to know what the other person has to say than to turn your meeting into a monologue.

Use orientation phrases: Use your imagination and your 5 senses to fascinate and seduce that person. Use positive anchors to tell a story or tell a scene. For example, "Imagine your best trip to the mountains, where the wind brings the smell of the forest and the rain."

Be attentive: Although it is never too much to captivate, first impressions go beyond physical appearance or the perfume you wear. Your kindness will be the best stamp you can leave on a person. Always converse by looking into the eyes, with your body subtly leaning towards the other person, and if he or she tells you something very intimate, don't hesitate to sit next to him or her, so that your real interest in them may be felt.

Persuading for a Promotion

I know the thought of walking into your boss's office, sitting down, and starting a conversation makes you sweat. That's it, how do you start this topic? Of course, you can rehearse in front of the mirror many times until the speech sounds convincing and you are confident, but you have to be realistic; maybe that persuasive script you wrote at home has some lines that may not work.

This is completely normal, and many people experience this. Before sending an email or message to your boss expressing that you want to talk to them about your professional future, I recommend you first clear your mind and think: Do you know what you want? Is it professional? If you are going to ask for a promotion, you need to answer this question and more.

In this section, I want to help you make this conversation as natural as possible and give you confidence in yourself and your abilities. I know that applying for a promotion is not easy, but by following a few tips, you can be prepared and leave with a smile on your face to succeed in your new role at your company. Maybe you'll get that promotion where you are named a software expert, something you've been hoping for a long time.

Why Are You Asking for that Promotion?

Some companies believe that frequent job changes are a phenomenon that must now be accepted. They are not wrong to a certain extent. While it's true that employees don't stay with the same company for decades, we may be overlooking certain aspects that could keep us on the job longer.

Frankly, frequent job changes are not only a problem for companies that need to recruit and train new professionals constantly, but also for employees. While it is a way to get promotions, pay raises, and career advancement, it involves taking risks in adapting to a new team or boss who may not be compatible with you and discovering that your job's environment and ins and outs may not work out.

In the worst-case scenario, you may wait for a job interview for a while, which can be exhausting. After all, it's been a long time since you've seen a recruiter for the first time, and those nerves you managed to control years ago will resurface.

For this reason, both employees and managers have a responsibility to discuss future career prospects. This gets you closer to the life and work you want; giving employers the information, they need to help you achieve those goals.

How do you apply for that promotion? Visualize what your journey through your current job has been like:

- How long have you been with the company? More than 2 years? 10 years? If you've only been for a few months, I recommend you spend a little more time demonstrating your value to the company in a better way. Maybe in 1 month, you're more prominent than others, but if you want to move to another level at this point, it's a bit rushed and harmful.

- What have you achieved during this period? Of course, you actively cooperate in your field, and your superiors congratulate you for it. What are your milestones within the company so far? For example, you may have acquired a high-value customer, helped develop software that boosted the company, built a team, or improved processes.

It is essential to answer these questions and be completely honest. Make a list of what you have done in the company, good and bad (no one is immune to some mistakes). Having a very clear idea of everything you are contributing and growing will help you communicate this to your boss. The more specific and quantifiable, the better.

This way, you will be able to provide your boss with reliable data about the importance of your work in the company. Show how good you are and, most importantly, exceed expectations in your field of work. After all, this is why you want to take on more challenges and improve yourself.

If you want to make this list more professional, you can use a strategy called the "briefcase technique."

While this technique is primarily aimed at freelancers, it's great for employees: it involves creating a multi-page proposal document in which you can show areas for improvement through job advancement. Once you've spoken to your boss and it's time to talk about salary, show this document and describe exactly how you will address the company's challenges in the areas mentioned above.

This will show your boss that you are not just interested in making more money, but that your goal is to be an essential part of the company and get good results. You will notice that you have spent some time analyzing the company's areas of opportunity and are willing to take responsibility for improving them. It will give you a good image.

To successfully apply for a promotion, you must determine what you want in your future career. Don't just say that you learned a lot during this time, but show those learnings and what most valuable elements they provide to the company.

When you are sure that you are doing well at work and know you need to move up the ladder in your field, you are ready to schedule the long-awaited conversation with your boss. Now, to successfully apply for a promotion, I recommend that you plan the meeting, so you know exactly what you'll be talking about. This doesn't mean you have to understand the scripts fully, but you can use some tricks while having this conversation.

Below, I show you some general guidelines on how to apply for job promotions so you can review them in detail. Take them into account to make the conversation with your boss more professional and effective, and get the promotion you deserve.

Identify That Position You Want

As I said earlier, you must be entirely sure of what you want in your future career before applying for that promotion. Many people apply for a promotion but can't find a field or position. Have you considered this aspect? What is the corporate structure of the company? You must make sure that you not only have the intention to move forward but that you have a place in the company to do so.

If a specific job opening is already available, this is a great advantage, as you only have to make an application. Otherwise, you and your boss may have to come up with a new role for you to fill. Creating a "new position" is not a ridiculous idea, it's your chance to show that you're ready to take on new responsibilities. When you speak with confidence, your boss will be able to see that you are a leader, ideal for tackling new projects and challenges.

Keep in Mind the Relationship You've Been Having With the Boss

If your relationship is good, you can be candid about your plans or uncertainties about the future of your professional development. The best managers know how to create or find opportunities that match their skills, interests, and challenges. Therefore, it is crucial to consider these factors before the conversation.

On the other hand, if the relationship with the boss is not ideal, or the boss does not have the authority to make such decisions, consider looking for another professional in a more senior position. Determine who to talk to, and whether or not they work in another department.

You Can Talk to Your Colleagues

Knowing why someone on your team left can help you think about your future and consider possible changes you may not have thought of. Also, if it's a job offer, you can find out the job details and, if you're interested, follow the steps below to apply.

Wait for the Right Time

If you're waiting for the perfect moment, you run the risk of wasting your time, but remember that some situations are better than others. For example, if your company is in crisis and your boss is trying to develop a strategy to deal with the situation, this is one of the worst times to talk. On the other hand, if you're taking advantage of it during a semi-annual or annual review of your field or position, it's an ideal time to address your career development.

I'll leave you with some other good ideas of which are good times and which are not so good times.

When can you approach asking for that promotion? Here are the signs:

- You notice that the company has had new changes, maybe they installed a series of servers, and you need a hand to make the best use of them.
- If your boss is going on vacation, it may be a good time (even if it sounds a bit funny and opportunistic). But surely, about two weeks before his break, he will be in a very good mood and will be able to consider your request more positively.
- If your area is focused on a large client or high-value business, what better way to show what you're worth?

When not to approach asking for promotions:
- Have you noticed that, unfortunately, they are laying off employees in different areas instead of opening new opportunities? Don't be discouraged, wait for the situation to stabilize and the company to have better days.
- If your company is going through a difficult time, instead of investing more, expenses increase. Even you and your colleagues have to go the extra mile to help the company succeed.
- They just lost a high-value customer or failed to close the deal despite all efforts.

Be Your Manager

Many managers want their teams to be proactive and able to solve problems on their own. If you find tasks that match your skills and interests with the unmet needs of your team, you may be able to create your promotions and corresponding positions. Explain why your idea worked and meet with your team or manager to discuss it. Make sure you get information about the company's future and how your project will be implemented after your manager's approval.

Research More About the Position You Want

A mandatory question in a conversation with your boss is how much money you want to make. This question is always a bit awkward, and you don't know if you are asking for more or fewer numbers, and you end up hurting yourself. However, so that this aspect doesn't catch you off guard, you can do some research with peers in similar positions.

Also, find out what kind of tasks you'll be performing and what your responsibilities might be. These factors will help you put clearer numbers on your desk.

Ask for Feedback

If you've had this conversation with your boss, ask them for their thoughts on your current job. You may discover details you hadn't noticed before. If everything goes better than you expected, they may even realize your value before you even expose it to them. Also, asking your boss for feedback will let them know that you're willing to listen and find new ways to grow. Don't put the whole conversation on you, but also listen to what he or she has to say. Remember: this is a conversation, not an exhibition.

Don't Make These Mistakes

As with best practices on how to apply for a promotion, some mistakes can put you in uncomfortable or damaging situations. Consider this basic list of common mistakes and avoid them at all costs, so your boss isn't left with a bad impression.

- **Being 100% sure you deserve that promotion:** Assuming the confidence, or worse, the arrogant attitude that you deserve a promotion will only end your conversation with your boss sooner than you think. You have to be confident but not lose your feet on the ground.
- **Be open-minded:** One thing to keep in mind — you are not the only employee in the company. Your boss manages more people who are just as valuable as you. If your boss doesn't agree that it is time to promote you at this time, listen to his or her reasons and look at it as a challenge to improve yourself.
- **Don't get mad if it doesn't go the way you expected:** Your presentation may have been impressive and the chemistry in the conversation may have been amazing. But if your boss doesn't think you can get a promotion yet, don't make the terrible mistake of getting angry and showing it. Not only will this attitude cause you to be passed over for future consideration, but it may even cost you your job if you lose your temper a little. Breathe and keep overcoming challenges.
- **Don't compare yourself to others:** Some employees recklessly compare their work to that of others to prove their worth. If your colleagues don't have the same challenge as you, that doesn't mean you have a duty to expose it. Go speak up for yourself and

your goals. Complaining about your coworkers will only give you a problematic image that your boss won't want to deal with. Show maturity that you are a team player, allowing everyone to improve their productivity and performance.

Persuading in a Job Interview

Just as asking for a promotion is key, it is also necessary for a job interview, so I dedicate this section to it.

You want to be more persuasive in some specific areas, but sometimes you don't know how to do it. The ability to persuade gives you a competitive advantage in different situations in life, such as in a job interview. It would be best to consider some keys so that the image you project is pleasing.

Knowing who you are talking to and paying attention to their body language is crucial to empathizing with the interviewer. If you extend your palm when you speak, it gives the impression that you are a straightforward person. A sincere smile will give you positivity and confidence, you will stand tall without being nervous, and you will move naturally.

Try to be consistent with the information he receives from you through your 5 senses: 80% of the visual attention you receive will be on your face, especially your expression. By ear, he will pick up on your speech's tone, volume, and speed. In greetings, whether with 2 kisses or handshakes, touch plays a vital role in providing a sense of security and maintaining an appropriate distance. Through our sense of smell, we can pick up the scent, perfume, and breath of another person.

It is vital to communicate your value proposition well: try to do the interviewer a favor and find a solution to one of their problems, so that they feel indebted and reciprocate with their kindness. If you rehearse for this situation, you will improve. Get to know the company on the Internet and let them know if you see flaws or innovations.

Acknowledge the strengths of the company and the interviewer's work there, albeit with good arguments. It turns out that compliments at the right time will delight the recipient and bring you closer to the other person.

In a conversation, try to strike a balance between logic and emotion. How you make the interviewer feel is as important as the information they get from you. Use the right adjectives to describe yourself, speak with passion, and turn those flaws into virtues. Provide vital facts about your career and what motivates you to execute the position.

Listening and reflection help build confidence in the interlocutor. We listen differently, depending on our mood, how we feel about the speaker, and what we think about what they are saying. Listening is important to ask relevant questions later.

Later, when we talk about body language and manipulation, you will be able to combine it with this and achieve a connection and persuasion that will give you that longed-for job.

Persuading to Connect With Your Venture

For every entrepreneur, sales are an important pillar of successful business growth. Here are 4 core ideas that can help you improve persuasion and sales.

Remember That You Must Always Believe in Your Venture

You must remember why you are doing what you are doing in the first place and what product or service you want to market.

Most likely, you have started a business to offer something; it may be a product or service to fill a void in someone else's life. Somehow, you want to make life better; don't forget that.

Think Like a Scientist

It is necessary to have a hypothesis to carry out a framework to evaluate the responses obtained in the experiment objectively.

That is, just like scientists, entrepreneurs can test their commercialization. For example, suppose an entrepreneur has two approaches for his next sales presentation or marketing plan but doesn't know which one to choose. In that case, he can eliminate one option with simple actions such as asking family and friends, but if he needs to dig deeper, he can conduct surveys, polls, and/or focus groups.

Do Social Testing

Social proof is anything that shows your audience that you have something in common and that you are part of a tribe that claims what you are selling. If entrepreneurs want to convince customers, it's important to include social proof in their conversations, and this can be done by mentioning how someone has recently invested in a product or service.

Focus on One Word

When starting a business, a useful exercise is to find a single word, that word that defines what you have. If you can't find it, you can ask friends, clients, and other people for help.

Persuading for Family Welfare

This is specific; it is about how you can persuade your family to get things from them so that they are better off. For example, you are in the process of securing a lease on a house, but the competition is challenging. You have someone in front of you who has already bet on placing the papers to get the property, but you and your family need it, so you persuade the real estate agent to see how they can put you among the first to get the property because it is close to your work, near the children's school, near a hospital to take the grandmother who is already sick, in short, you persuade to achieve your personal goal.

Persuading for Social Welfare

Similar to the previous point, but with social welfare, this is everything you can do to improve the community where you live. Perhaps persuade the people in your building to create a walkway for dogs to pass through, possibly lead the group and convince them to remove some pet restrictions that have made coexistence more difficult.

In short, it is any persuasive action that aims to help the community.

However, not everything that is manipulation and dark psychology is good all the time, as I have shown you so far. There are bad actions, and I will tell you a bit about them in another chapter.

Chapter 3: Psychological Manipulation Techniques

I hope that you know how to start using persuasion to your advantage with the previous chapter. Now, moving down to somewhat darker scenarios, I want to show you how dark psychology works. These are manipulation techniques that occur daily on many different spectrums, at home, in marital or parent-child relationships, in the workplace, and many places.

The techniques below each have their characteristics and are part of different manipulators, and have different consequences on the victims.

Guilt

Guilt is one of the strongest emotions and the most mobilizing for human beings. For the vast majority of people, guilt is an unmanageable experience because it arises from childhood and is related to everyone's morals, family morals, and social morals.

Generally, when a person feels guilty, they become restless and need to correct the cause of the emotion as soon as possible to restore balance. This urge to stop feeling guilty makes people more fickle, so guilt will be one of the emotions exploited in manipulation techniques.

Another way to create this is to use phrases like "you should do," "you should have" to make them feel guilty and ashamed of the other person because they feel uncomfortable and can do what they are supposed to do. Even though something tells them that deep down they may not agree, they do it anyways.

Insecurity

Insecurities about ourselves will be another emotion that will play a decisive role in manipulation.

It is not that confident people cannot be manipulated, and it is not that all abused people are distrustful. Still, a good manipulator knows how to discover everyone's weaknesses and exploits them to the maximum for their benefit.

A good observer knows where each person is most sensitive, and they can create a state of confusion or insecurity in that person simply by saying the right word, which will make him or her more receptive to what the other person is communicating.

They may also use criticism, weaving lies, or whatever to make fun of you or tease you (make you feel guilty or ashamed) at work, in front of others, friends, family, etc., to make you feel guilty or embarrassed.

Compassion

Having empathy or pity for others is one of the basic keys to getting what you want. That poor person will make you end up doing something you don't want to do, relieve your guilt of living a life with more abundance or simply want to do something for them and thus they take advantage of you.

Boosting the Ego

One technique often effective in getting what a person wants is to boost another person's ego through compliments (false or real), which makes them feel comfortable with the manipulator, valued by the manipulator, and ultimately like what they hear.

If they end up relying on this compliment, they will put their self-esteem in the hands of another person and not in their own hands, depending on the image that the other person gives them back; in this case, influenced by what the manipulator tells them.

At the same time, they don't usually go unnoticed; they become very generous in helping or giving gifts; it's a strategy. Then they ask you to do other things that they need based on the gift. They can be charming, kind, and good people. The problem is that it is usually an appearance, and what matters most to them is what a person can do for them.

Subtle Intimidation

One of the key characteristics of a good move is stealth or subtlety. Language is broad, rich and unknowingly marks us from the inside, which is why the words used are so important.

Fear is an inherently human emotion, and generating this feeling in the human body is the perfect weapon to create doubt or tend to listen for solutions when its effects begin to manifest, such as pain or fear.

In addition, attention is paid to the importance of language in these situations, as sometimes the appeal is not to individuality but to the group's welfare and its impact on peers, family, or the manipulator himself. "Don't do it for yourself, do it for us (for your children, for your peers, etc.)."

It must also be said that sometimes it is not so subtle. It is manipulated through fear, threats, and coercion. If you don't do what you say, do it at your own risk. They do not respect anyone's freedom of decision; manipulators mark what to do.

Discord

Manipulators are usually popular and create a certain amount of attraction in others. Hence, people tend to pay attention to them when they talk, and the confidence they have in doing so usually builds trust, so if they start to be on each other. What happens when they create discord? It gives them credibility.

There is nothing more lucrative to get your wish than to create discord among others and become a manipulative figure while they are involved in self-created battles.

You just have to pick the person and make them doubt themselves by showing them an interpretation of reality that is dismissive and unrealistic but will make them look weird in front of colleagues (for example), be more reticent, marginalized, sarcastic, and in the end, they get shut down. In the long run, he will feel that the manipulator is the only one accompanying him; he will be afraid of being alone and of being left out of the situation.

Playing the Fool

Manipulative people are usually not stupid at all, but there is nothing like acting stupid, incompetent, or poor. Unfortunately, people don't realize it, so they demand less of them or forgive them for their mistakes.

Lies by Omission

The best way to lie is not to make up a side story that you can forget but to leave something out, modifying small details of the story to create ambiguity or subtly changing the subject so that the other person forgets what is being discussed.

Another way is to drag out answers and make them so grotesque that they eventually stop paying attention because it doesn't get to the heart of the question and tells a story instead of a definitive answer.

Emotional Blackmail

Emotional blackmail is one of the most obvious manipulation techniques and sometimes does not contain subtle messages on its own.

Think of the "if you leave me, I'll kill myself" relationship. Noticeably, we are dealing with a manipulation technique based on direct emotional blackmail, which may or may not positively affect the manipulator.

Gaslighting

"Gaslighting" is a pattern of emotional abuse in which victims are manipulated to question their perceptions, judgments, or memories. This can make people feel anxious, confused, and even depressed.

The word comes from the Hollywood classic "Gaslight," in which a man manipulates his wife into believing she is insane and thus steals her hidden wealth. He hides objects (paintings, jewelry) to convince his wife that she is responsible, even though she doesn't remember. It will also dim the gas lamp fire (there is no electricity), making you believe that it still shines as brightly as before.

Of course, this makes the protagonist feel like she is going crazy; she doesn't want to leave the house, or she is anxious and crying constantly. The husband warns her that he will leave the relationship and threatens to send her to the doctor for medication or hospitalization. Of course, the abuser knows exactly what he is doing, and if it weren't for the investigators to decipher the situation and unmask the thief, he would have almost succeeded.

While the movie shows an extreme case, this manipulative technique is used consciously or unconsciously in relationships. I will show you some scenarios.

For example, you can say:

- When you say "you hurt me," and the abuser says, "I never said that; you're imagining it," he started sowing the seed of doubt.

It could also go like this:

- "I feel bad when you do that," to which the abuser replies, "you're sensitive; it's just a joke." He tried to convince you that it was a misunderstanding.

- Similarly, you may fight and defend yourself and still get the same words, "You overreacted," "You created a storm in a glass of water," or "You have paranoia," etc. So, instead of continuing to confront or pull away, you allow the doubts in you to be the basis of the relationship and seek approval from your partner or family.

This type of manipulation is very subtle but dangerous because it can lead us to continue with toxic relationships, be they love, work, or friendships, believing that we do have problems, being insecure, and relying on the opinions of others. It can also push us away from our loved ones to fear being confronted about their relationship.

These are the main effects in the medium and long term that cause the person who lacks criteria to make decisions on their own:

- **Doubts of their ability to remember:** This technique makes the victim doubt the functioning of their memory because the manipulative person convinces them to remember things that did not happen.

- **Doubts about their reasoning:** This makes the victim not trust their reasoning and make decisions, so they seek help in the judgment of others and especially in the manipulative person, which makes them see their mistakes.
- **Doubts about their mental health:** In extreme cases, the victim assumes that they have a psychological disorder that explains the inadequate emotional reactions or ways of thinking that are far from reality.
- **It affects their self-esteem:** All this is reflected in how self-esteem goes to the ground.

Positive Reinforcement

Positive reinforcement is a resource widely used in the field of psychology to reward those actions or behaviors for being reinforced and consolidated and is also used to manipulate. It provides some kind of reward or recognition to encourage the person to repeat the desired behavior.

This technique is often used in certain fields, such as education, different types of psychology, or in the workplace, among others.

With this type of resource, the purpose is to repeat and reinforce the desired behavior. For example, if someone is afraid to drive, getting into the car gradually and adding positive reinforcement, such as words of encouragement, can go a long way toward repeating and reinforcing the behavior.

With positive reinforcement, a relationship can be established between the behavior and the goals that can be achieved after the performance. For example, if a child does not like vegetables, but is rewarded for eating them, this behavior may increase.

These are the characteristics:

- **Apply the behavior:** You can strengthen a person's behavior, by achieving that, through positive reinforcement, repeating more often, and consolidating it.

- **Use pleasant rewards:** Positive stimuli are incentives obtained through positive reinforcement. For example, words of encouragement and motivation or a reward such as a gift or a gesture of kindness motivate someone to practice the desired behavior.

- **Use it appropriately:** Positive reinforcement should be used in specific situations and where it is needed. Behaviors should be reinforced with positive and motivating stimuli to encourage those who practice them. In this way, the correct association will be made, and positive reinforcement should always be given after implementing the behavior. You should watch for the person to do it, and there you reinforce, and you will see that they will repeat it.

Types of positive reinforcement

- **Natural reinforcement:** This type of positive reinforcement occurs when the person is doing something that provides natural gratification. For example, if a person wants to lose weight and looks at his or her diet, they will notice that they feel better and will lose pounds. If you flatter them at that moment, you will get points and get more attention.

- **Social Reinforcement:** Reinforcement is given by society and externally to reinforce the mother's behavior. For example, you congratulate your partner because he or she brought the coffee to your desk, as you had been encouraging them for days.
- **Personal Reinforcement:** This can also include positive reinforcement that a person can generate on their own. The way a person talks and motivates themselves to cheer up before something is also positive reinforcement. For example, the way you encourage yourself before you go in to ask for the promotion, as I showed you above.
- **Tangible reinforcement:** Implicit positive reinforcement through rewards or in-kind rewards, for example, money or gifts.

Positive Reinforcement Examples

There are many examples, as I have been showing you. What matters is that what it does is that the behavior is associated with something good and is repeated and consolidated over time.

For example, if an employee in the sales department has achieved outstanding results for the company and the company gives him a salary bonus or trip each time, that will be a positive reinforcement. This reward will encourage him to continue striving for the best possible results.

We always think of positive reinforcement as a good thing, but when used with evil, it can also be used to manipulate. The truth is that we have all used positive reinforcement in one way or another. Parents use it to make children behave, teachers use it to make students more eager to study, bosses use it to encourage productivity, and associates use it to modify behavior with others. It is an integral part of our interactions, but it only becomes a problem when it goes wrong.

Positive reinforcement is when a good or wanted stimulus is presented in a way that appears to be a consequence of a behavior. An example is a child who doesn't like to eat vegetables and gets a bar of chocolate if he does. This registers in your mind that the two items are related. An employee who works hard and becomes more productive, in the end, gets a bonus. The brain makes the connection between hard work and additional income the next time they have to do the same thing. They will have that positive feeling or reward from the previous time and will take a course of action that helps get a similar result.

If manipulators use positive efforts, they do so to have things that benefit them. For example, an abusive person may buy a gift after a significant abusive event to avoid being reported. You may have heard of those men who beat their wife and bring her flowers the next day. In those cases, the abuser wants her to accept the abuse as a norm that comes with a gift. The message he gives is that if you keep quiet, you have a good thing going.

Positive reinforcement is used when they want you to be obedient or when they want to take advantage of you. Machiavellians are good at using this, for example, the programming boss who has embezzled money and rewards you in exchange for your silence. Manipulators often use this reinforcement to get you to do things against your will. The goal is to lull you to sleep, and they know that when they succeed, they can advance and grow in their purposes.

Silent Treatment

Silent therapy is a manipulative technique used by manipulators as a form of punishment. It includes avoiding any communication with you and is associated with a cold and distant attitude. They ignore you and pretend you do not exist. **This treatment can be of 2 types:**

1   **Silent treatment:** They stay at home but do not talk to you. Occasionally, they give you a cold, intimidating, disapproving look and remain silent with an expression of indifference. You will see them chatting politely with other people, other family members, or visitors on the phone to emphasize their attitude towards you. It can last for hours, sometimes even one or several days.

2   **Distant silence:** They leave the house and go somewhere else without saying a word to you. They disappear for hours, days, or even weeks and do not answer calls or messages. They suddenly stop communicating with you. They use this punishment when, according to their confused thinking, when you do something they don't like or make a comment, they see it as criticism of them in their opinion. They use it deliberately to warn you of the consequences of your actions and educate you to be more obedient.

What Do They Do With the Silent Treatment?

It is a manifestation of power, and they play on your fear of abandonment to show you that they can live without you. They test your limits and see how far they can push you. They degrade and objectify you and make you feel useless. **By doing this, they succeed:**

- Have attention from you and make you worry and wonder what you did wrong. They seek to get you to go after them, ask them to come back, cry, and show that you are suffering because of that fight or upset.
- They manipulate you to do what they want or stop doing that thing that makes them so uncomfortable.
- They test limits and see how far they can go; if the first absence lasted a week, the other one will be longer so that you think they will not come back.

Intimidation

Because manipulators aim to dominate at all costs and be seen as righteous, they often use aggression. This category deals with the more aggressive tactics often used by narcissists.

Such methods include provocation, harassment, and intimidation, where the narcissist points at you, calls you out, yells, acts emotionally, intentionally hurts you, blatantly lies, threatens, or even attacks you personally. Not only that, but they turn it around and act like they are reacting or ignoring you, and you are the one who is irrational, overly emotional, and aggressive towards them.

Yelling

This is a manipulation technique that is done for a reason: it makes you feel afraid or uncomfortable to the point of complying with whatever they want you to do. Manipulators use yelling in two ways to persuade others. People yell to dominate or to play the victim and gain your sympathy.

Yelling can be used to intimidate a person. When a manipulative person yells at you, they may be seeking to scare you because they probably want you to be afraid.

Manipulators resort to yelling, it's the way they act because they know you have no logical arguments to get you to do what they want. They know that if you stick to the facts of the matter, you can get away with it, so they yell because they want to throw you off balance and make you lose the argument. When a person raises their voice in an argument, it is a sign of growing hostility, but it is also a sign that they are passionate about the issue they are arguing about.

You need to evaluate the yelling to understand if he is using this to manipulate you. Just as with other manipulation techniques, you have to look at the person's intention; when manipulators yell, they play a victim role in an interaction, usually, not always, and they choose to do so in front of others. When a person yells at you in a public space, those who pass by and see that they don't have the full story of what is going on will assume you are wrong and put you on the spot, perhaps forcing you to accept what that person says so you don't continue in that embarrassing scenario.

Persistency

Persistence can translate into nagging or bullying. It is a way of manipulating that makes the other person do something, even though he or she previously denied doing it or agreed to it at the time. Persistence is an interaction in which the person makes a repeated request while the other ignores it many times. Although it has negative connotations, persistence is an integral part of interpersonal communication in many social dynamics. Parents nag children to do some things; indeed, persistence is required when training children to pick up some good habits. It can be used with good intentions; friends or relatives may ask you to do things to help you. Moreover, some persistence is needed in healthy relationships. People with dark personality traits may be persistent in getting you to do things that affect you and benefit them.

If you want to know if the person who insists has bad intentions, you have to examine the person's situation. If they ask you to do something that benefits them, the persistence can look blunt, or you can detect threats or anger in their body language, and what they say. If they are trying to guilt you into doing something you don't want to do, if you are repeatedly asked to do a job in the office, it may be that the person is a bit controlling, though not necessarily that they are mean. When people with bad intentions nag you, there is usually an "otherwise..." in what they are asking you to do, and if you look at the fine print, you realize it is more of a demand than a request.

Isolation

We all have social support systems that help us deal with complex situations that prevent all bad decisions. We have peers, friends, and family that notice when our behavior changes or when we start hanging out with bad people, and they have our back. Manipulators know this, and one of the things they do when they want to change you is to isolate you from your environment.

Isolation makes it easier for them to abuse; it eliminates resources you might have when you start to be abused. It closes off avenues of escape and increases the feeling of helplessness. The abuser makes sure that there is no one to rescue you when things go sideways. The power increases and their control over the victim makes him or her more dependent on the abuser. It isolates the victim from the outside world and is widely used by all kinds of manipulators. When a cult leader tries to indoctrinate young people, he makes sure they are locked in to control them with the information they give him. The same thing happens in abusive relationships, bullying at work, and many other spaces.

When the abuser seeks to isolate you, they start by driving a wedge between you and the people close to you. They will learn all about the dynamics between your family and friends and use this to exploit weaknesses in the relationship to sow mistrust and conflict. For example, if a man knows you are close to a sister, but you have unresolved childhood issues with her, he may rekindle those conflicts so that you begin to pull away. In the workspace, a manipulator may create enmities between you and colleagues so that they get angry and stop siding with you and being with you. If you join a cult group or sect, and the leader is manipulative, he or she may insist that you cut ties with friends and family and rely only on other members of the group.

In business rivalries, at work, and even in your personal life, they can isolate you by slandering your name and taking credit away from others on the site. As they say, "Divide and conquer" is a way to isolate you that is used by people who have Machiavellian traits. In this case, the manipulator uses isolation as a double-edged sword to control you, and when he succeeds, he takes the abuse to the next level because he knows you have no one else to turn to. Other manipulation strategies such as gaslighting work best when you have been isolated.

They say love is blind, and sometimes, in relationships, you are blind to the traits that happen with the person you are dating. Many manipulators may seek to isolate you from the first moment they meet you. If you start dating a person and notice that they never want to hang out around the house or don't want you to make friends on casual dates, they probably want to isolate you so that you can't have friends give an objective assessment of their character.

In workspaces, isolation can come in many forms: a person can isolate you if they deny you access to opportunities, withhold important information from you or keep you in the dark about crucial issues to job performance. A manipulative person can use isolation to punish you if you don't do what they want. For example, they may invite friends and acquaintances to a meeting but not invite you, so that you feel left out and are forced to do just what he or she wants so that you will have an invitation to the next meeting.

Facts Manipulation

This is another effective technique because it is based on facts that are subject to interpretation. If a person manipulates facts, technically, they are not lying, they are just using the facts to their advantage. It may involve selecting some episodes, lying some points, or taking them out of context; even the most disputed facts are subject to interpretation, and people with bad personality traits are good at coming up with interpretations that portray them in the best possible light.

Machiavellians are skilled at using this information to turn bad things into things that seem good. One way to manipulate facts in interpersonal meetings is to make excuses. People can make excuses for bad behaviors by creating narratives that distort the context of the objectionable actions taken. Another way to manipulate the facts is to blame the victim for causing the victimization.

In many cases, abusers can convince the victim to do things to make them feel they deserve the abuse. Many batterers who hit their wives defend themselves by saying that she made them do it. It is a manipulative technique that works effectively after the prey has been cut off from her support system. Victims who are in love with or dependent on the abuser are more likely to accept distorted interpretations or dependence on the abuser and are more likely to get distorted interpretations of abusive events because judgment is affected by affection for the abuser.

Withholding information is another common technique involving the manipulation of facts. Someone may tell the truth with the intent to convince. Manipulators know that the reaction to a piece of information depends on the mood the person is in when they receive the information or whether they will consider it a priority when they receive it. Manipulators also know that withholding some key details can affect how information is digested and reacted to.

Timely disclosures and withholding details are essential. When you have information that could damage your public image, but you have a legal obligation to disclose it, you often do so at the close of business on Fridays, when many people are looking forward to the weekend and not paying attention to announcements. This ensures that bad information does not get much media coverage.

Mind Control and Mind Games

The term mind control has many definitions and interpretations, but the key thing to remember is that it does not imply any magical or supernatural ability; it just requires a basic understanding of human emotions and behavior. Mind control can include brainwashing a person, re-educating them, reshaping their mind, and using coercive techniques to persuade them to accept certain things. Mind control comes in many forms, and I could write a book about all of them, but I will show you the concept in general terms for our purposes. It occurs when one person tries to make another person feel, think, or act a certain way, or react and make decisions according to a particular pattern. It can be a woman trying to make her boyfriend acquire certain habits or a cult leader trying to convince their followers that they are God.

Mind control is based on one thing: information. We own the thoughts and beliefs we have because we learn them. When we consciously and constantly receive new information, it has the potential to change our beliefs, thoughts, and even memories. The brain is programmed for survival, so it is very good at learning information critical to our survival. When you keep receiving certain information, your brain starts to believe it even if it knows it is not true. For example, even if you are the most rational person, if you watch 100 online videos about a conspiracy theory, you will start to believe it to some extent. This explains why seemingly intelligent people are indoctrinated into cults or even terrorist groups.

However, if you want to have control over others, hopefully not with bad intentions, it cannot be achieved if you do not have control of your emotions. That is why in the next chapter, I will talk about emotional influence, and later in another chapter, I will explain how to have emotional intelligence.

Chapter 4: Emotional Influence

Manipulating, persuading, convincing, and using the tools in this book, for better or worse, cannot be accomplished if you don't first work on your inner self. It's like taking a car in bad condition to drive all over the United States. If you want to take the interstate, you have to have a vehicle in good condition.

If you want to manipulate, you have to work on your emotions and feel confident inside yourself to use them when you communicate with others. The result, if you don't do it, is that as soon as you get in front of the person you want to influence, they will disarm you with some argument and now you will look weak or even manipulated if they have better emotional intelligence than you; that is precisely why I describe these concepts below.

Manage Your Emotions

The first thing you have to do to control and manage your emotions is to know them.

Invest the time you need to identify them and understand what emotions they provoke when facing different situations in your work and personal life. Recall how you behaved in a given situation and reflect on how you would like to behave. Did you take defensive measures during that conflict with a colleague? Are you silent in conversations with your boss? Make a list of these behaviors and think about how to deal with them next time.

Emotional intelligence, a topic I will address later, helps you control and better manage your nerves.

There are two types of people: The first type of people blocks when nerves overcome them in a situation because they interpret those nerves as something negative, as a warning signal or a warning from the body to get out of there. Another group interprets these nerves as excitement and a desire to do good: a sign of motivation that can make your presentations, meetings, or job interviews a success. Which group do you belong to? You can work on your emotional intelligence, either alone or in a group.

If emotional intelligence is a great advantage and benefit for you... imagine it for the whole team! Emotional intelligence seeks to increase trust among members, identification with the group, and its effectiveness. It is the perfect tool for the group's objectives to exceed expectations. Learn how to improve relationships with your colleagues.

Although self-esteem cannot be left out, that is the basis for you to have your emotions controlled and clear.

Emotionally intelligent people trust themselves as much as they trust others. He is the one who learns to express his feelings clearly and is committed to learning from others. That is to value the ideas of others and not be afraid to expose their ideas.

Set Your Goals: What Do You Want to Emotionally Influence Others for?

You have to be sure of what you want to influence other people for. Maybe it is because you want to get a promotion at work, you are in a transformation process where you want to show yourself as a leader.

Maybe until now, because of the personality you have, introverted, quiet, you have not caused any impact wherever you go. You feel you deserve to grow as a person, achieve better goals, and be a better version of yourself. You want to stand out, and that is your plan, or maybe you have plans to manipulate others for your dark purposes. Whatever your goal is, you need to be clear about why you are doing this.

The reason is so that you can be clear about the objectives of what you will do from here on out, whether it is to manipulate someone else, grow in the work environment, become an operations manager, or become that woman who likes to be in control, people will notice you because you transformed yourself. Whatever it is, be clear about this before you start the manipulation process.

Emotional Influencing Techniques

Before we begin, it is important to note that none of these methods are designed to influence other people with bad intentions. Nothing is included here that would be harmful to someone in any way, especially their self-esteem. These are ways to win friends and influence people to use psychology positively, without making others feel bad. I have already shown you strategies to manipulate with bad intentions, and later I will show you others.

The Benjamin Franklin Effect

Getting someone to do us a favor can be complicated. Doing so is known as the Benjamin Franklin effect. Legend has it that when Franklin was in the Pennsylvania Legislature, an opponent who had spoken against him (Franklin did not name him) was a very influential man. Franklin was very disturbed by this opposition and hostility and decided to win the support of this gentleman. What he came up with was very curious and clever. Instead of doing this person a favor or a service, he enticed him to do him a favor and borrowed a very rare book from his library.

The gentleman in question lent it to him immediately, and Franklin returned it to him a week later with a note thanking him for the favor.

When they met again in Parliament, the gentleman spoke to him very politely (something he had never done before). The man had been willing to help Franklin ever since, and they became good friends, a friendship that lasted until his death. This fact proves the truth of an adage Franklin learned as a child, "You are more likely to get another helping hand from someone who has already helped you than from someone who owes you."

There is another example in Dostoevsky's *The Brothers Karamazov* that is very illustrative of this phenomenon. Fyodor Pavlovitch recalls that in the past, he was asked why he hated someone so much. He replied, "I'll tell you. He didn't hurt me. I got dirty with him, and I hated him ever since." Just as we get a vicious cycle in these examples, the Benjamin Franklin effect shows that a virtuous cycle can emerge.

The scientists decided to test the theory and found that those whom the researchers had asked for personal help rated it much better than the other groups. It seems contradictory because common sense tells us that we help those we like and annoy those we dislike. But the reality seems to be that we tend to like people who are nice to us, not those who are rude or mean to us.

Ask a Lot

The trick is to start by asking for much more than we want or need and then reduce our requirements. Start by making an important request to someone which is likely to be denied. Then quickly turn around and ask for something less expensive, which was actually what we wanted in the first place. This trick may also seem counterintuitive, but the idea is that even if it is unreasonable, the person who rejects our first request will feel bad, so when a reasonable request is made, they will feel more overwhelmed and obligated to do so it.

Using the Person's Name

Using a person's name or title depending on the situation is another tool for gaining trust. Dale Carnegie, the author of *How to Win Friends and Influence People,* explains that using someone's name is very important and effective in building friendships. It is said that a person's name is the sweetest sound for that person in any language. Our name is a fundamental part of our identity, so hearing it validates our existence and makes us feel more positive about the person who validates us. Using titles or nicknames can also have a powerful effect. This can be as simple as every time we see an acquaintance and call them "friend" or "colleague," or calling someone we want to work with "boss," as cliché as it may sound, it works in practice.

Flattery

Flattery opens many doors. This may seem obvious at first, but we must keep in mind some important caveats. First, it is essential to know that it can do more harm than good if it is not considered sincere. Researchers looked at the motivations and responses behind flattery and found something very important: it seems that people tend to seek cognitive balance, always trying to keep their thoughts and feelings on a similar level. So, if we flatter someone with a lot of self-esteem and sincerity, they will love it because it validates their feelings. However, if we praise someone with low self-esteem, it can backfire because it interferes with how people perceive them. Of course, this does not mean that we should belittle a person with low self-esteem.

The Mirroring Technique

Mirroring, also known as pantomime or mirroring technique, is something that some people do naturally. People with this ability are considered "chameleons;" they try to mimic their environment by imitating behavior, gestures, and even speech. However, this ability can also be used consciously and is a good technique to appear friendlier. The researchers studied imitation and found that those who were imitated were more likely to show a favorable impression of those who imitated them.

Even more interesting was their second finding that those whose behavior was imitated by others seemed more interesting and likable to others. This happens because imitating someone else's behavior makes you feel recognized. This recognition was positively associated with higher self-esteem and self-confidence, greater happiness, and better character toward others.

Offers You Can't Refuse

It includes starting with requests they cannot refuse. This is a reverse of the "aim high" technique, not with a big request, but with a small one. Once someone agrees to help us or agrees with us, they are more likely to be more willing to meet larger demands. Scientists tested this phenomenon in advertisements. They started by asking people to express their support for the environment and the rainforest, an elementary request. Then, they found that once someone agreed to support the environment, it was much easier to convince them to buy products that supported the rainforest and other things.

Know How to Correct

Correcting people when they make mistakes is not a good idea. Carnegie also pointed out in his famous book that telling others they are wrong is often unnecessary and alienates others from us. In reality, there are better ways to express disagreement and turn it into a polite conversation without telling them they were wrong because it touches on their self-centeredness. The idea behind this is simple: instead of arguing, listen to what they have to say and try to understand how they feel and why. Then find out what you have in common with them and use that as a starting point to explain your position. This makes the other person more likely to listen to you and allows you to correct them without losing ground.

Repeat

Repeating back what our interlocutor has just said is one of the most positive ways to influence others because we show our empathy by demonstrating that we understand what they are saying and how they feel. One of the most effective ways to do this is to interpret what they said and repeat it back, also known as reflective listening. Research shows that people tend to show more emotions and develop better therapeutic relationships when counselors use reflective listening. This can be deflected by talking to our friends. They feel more comfortable talking to us if we listen to what they have to say and rephrase it as a question to confirm that we understand. They also show more kindness and are more likely to listen to what we have to say because it shows we care about them.

Nod

Nod when they talk to you, especially when they help you. Scientists have found that when people nod while listening, they are more likely to agree with each other. They also find that when someone nods in front of us frequently, we do the same. This is understandable, as humans are known to mimic behaviors, especially those that are considered positive. So, if you want to be very persuasive, nod regularly during the conversation. The person you're talking to will find it hard not to nod and will start to vibe pleasantly about what's being said without even knowing it.

Chapter 5: Mind Control

A rather complex and controversial topic is mind control, controlling our minds, which is linked to the previous chapter, and controlling others. This is one of the tools that manipulators use to achieve their goals. It borders very close to brainwashing, which I will address later.

In this chapter, I will describe what mind control is and how it works.

What Is Mind Control?

Mind control seems to be related to superpowers, such as telepathy or the ability to control the minds of others. But mind control is when we become aware of our thoughts and emotions so that they do not dictate our behavior.

When our mind control is poor, we may regret some of the actions we did, for example, arguing with our partner, saying things we didn't mean, and at a certain point, when anger overpowers us, it may seem real. Instead, when we think coldly, we realize that emotions have taken over us.

Mind control is a set of techniques or habits that allow us to better understand our own emotions and thoughts, as well as those of others. Thus, it allows us to regulate our behavior and then control the behavior of others.

How to Mentally Control Others

Perhaps you have ever imagined using your mind to control others. Maybe you have even tried telepathy with null results.

The human mind is too complex to understand fully, let alone manage so easily. Yet hundreds of studies have found common patterns in most human behaviors. In much of what has been discovered, these tricks keep popping up. It turns out that certain stimuli (almost) always lead to the same result. Dare you give it a try?

Wisdom From a Parent

If you want people to take what you tell them more seriously, tell them it's what you learned from your dad. Without knowing it, people are more inclined to trust their dad's advice.

Words of Condition

If you want to have fun, try the following. When you're talking to a person, pick a word and nod every time they say it. It can be smiling, nodding your head, or saying a positive word (like "of course"). After a while, you will see that person saying the word more and more often without realizing it.

Always Win With Rock-Paper-Scissors

You should know this trick if you want to be the rock-paper-scissors world champion. Just before the game starts, ask your opponent a difficult question. Even better if they are a bit burdened.

Faced with this situation, the person becomes defensive and may opt for the scissors.

The Broccoli Trick

This trick designed for parents can be used in hundreds of situations. The original text reads:

If you want your kids to eat broccoli, ask them if they want two or five broccoli, not if they want it. That way, you decide for them and they will eat the broccoli, but they feel they can also decide by choosing the amount. You can replicate this in any situation: Instead of giving someone two choices, one that you like and one that you don't, give them two options that you like. They'll be happy to have a choice, and you'll win too.

Line-of-Sight Detector

Do you ever feel like someone is looking at you, but you can't catch them at the right moment? This trick is foolproof.

Give another big yawn when you think that person is looking at you. Then look at that person. Since yawning is contagious, if they yawn behind you, chances are they are looking at you.

Help "Take Off" a Theme Song

If a friend can't stop singing the same part of the song repeatedly, try this: sing the song's end to them. According to research, when we can't get a musical track out of our heads, thinking about its ending closes the infinite loop and allows another song to come in.

Be Attractive

Finally, apply double tricks with someone you like.

When holding hands, you make sure it's not cold no matter the circumstances. Warm hands are more comfortable and provide greater security.

Also, during a date, try to imitate some of the other person's movements and gestures (subtly, of course, so they don't think you're joking). This subconsciously builds confidence and makes them feel like a good fit.

This is a way to achieve (or not allow) mind control over a person. It's about how to change behavior. Remember, when behavior modification techniques are applied lovingly, carefully, and consistently, the person will change their behavior without resentment. However, if these techniques are applied incorrectly, the human mind can be damaged.

This is the key to the matter: the theory of cognitive dissonance. The three components are: behavioral control, thought control, and emotion control. Each of these components has a powerful effect on the other 2: change one and the others tend to follow. When the three of them change, the subject changes radically. We can summarize it this way: if you alter a person's behavior, their thoughts and feelings change to minimize dissonance (the discomfort that comes from feeling dissonance). To wit: When there is an issue between thoughts, feelings, and actions, those in conflict change to minimize the struggle.

In any type of totalitarianism, people create dissonance to exploit and control them. In addition to these three components, you can add another very important element: information control. By controlling the information people receive, you can manage and limit a person's ability to think for themselves. Let's look at each of them.

Types of Control

Behavioral Control

This includes controlling where you live, what you eat, clothing, sleep, work, rituals, etc. You have to make a very demanding plan with your people. They always have something to do. If you can control your actions, their heart and mind will follow.

Thought Control

The person must internalize the truth (your truth). Filter the information by beliefs, which will help you regulate how you think about information. This normalizes the way people think and creates a big barrier between them and others (outsiders, other people). Use techniques to stop thinking; there are several ways: have them recite a psalm, meditate, sing, concentrate on prayer, repeat a slogan or phrase, etc. The use of these technologies short-circuits the brain, preventing contact with reality. Let people see the group only in a positive light. If there is a problem, hold the member accountable and work hard.

Emotional Control

You have to manipulate people's feelings. Use guilt and fear to maintain control. Be confident that your group members will not notice the controls because of guilt, and will gradually adjust them, so they can examine themselves when things go wrong and thank you when you point out violations.

They use fear to manipulate in two ways: the first is by creating an external enemy (us vs. them) to pursue. Another is the fear of being punished by the leaders if you are not good enough. Good enough means staying true to the ideology. Remember, the most powerful emotional control is the fear of being left out. At the thought of leaving the group, a person has a panic reaction. People must find it almost impossible to conceive of any way of life outside the group. Do not point physical weapons at their heads; psychological weapons are equally and possibly more powerful.

Information Control

Deprive people of the information they need to face their trials, and they will be unable to do so. If you deny them access to the critical information needed to assess the situation, you can shape it to your purposes. Let the psychological chains on their hearts keep them out of society.

Totalitarianism

It means all or nothing (those who are not with me are against me). Remember, mind control is the process of uprooting beliefs and constructing new ones through coercive persuasion. It is a process aimed at ending people's independence and individuality and implanting their ideology. Chinese people call this type of ideological reform "brainwashing." A topic that I will show you later on, by the way.

- **Brainwashing:** Brainwashing is considered a different process from thought transformation or mind control. The difference is that the enemy does brainwashing, and people know who they are.

● **Thought control:** Thought control is more cunning. Victims do not see the people who change them as enemies because they see them as best friends and only as people with good intentions. Remember, manipulating people with guilt and pain makes it easier to get people to do what you want.

In the process, you will be able to re-educate the person to let go of the commandments they have learned in life and exchange them for the truth you provide. It may take a variable amount of time, but in this way, you will completely change the personality of your victim; even their family will not be able to identify them.

Remember, eight psychological aspects are the most important to reform thinking. They are all very important. Each is based on absolutist philosophical positions and mobilizes the polarizing emotional tendencies of the individual. Keep in mind that the psychological aspects, philosophical positions, and polarizing tendencies are interdependent, creating an atmosphere full of emotion and energy.

1. Control of the Environment and Communication

Diffusion control is the first task of reforming people's minds. You have to control everything you see, hear, read, write, experience, and express. You must exclude everything that is not your beliefs or the beliefs of your group.

Your organization must appear omniscient. You seem to have to know everything that is happening or is about to happen. Knowledge of reality is unique to you. In this environment, the individual is deprived of external information and internal reflection to check facts and maintain a degree of identity separate from the environment.

2. Mystical Manipulation

The mysteries of the organization. This attempts to elicit specific behavioral or emotional patterns that seem to arise spontaneously from the environment. For you, this must have an almost mystical quality. You must show a strong sense of purpose and demonstrate that you are the keeper of the truth. Followers must, in turn, create an atmosphere of mystery around corporations, parties, governments, guerrillas, paramilitaries, armies, and cults, convincing the followers that they are the chosen ones to carry out mysterious orders. The need to convey this mystery overcomes all decent considerations of immediate happiness. Remember, the end justifies the means. You must lie, cheat or do anything else to anyone outside your organization. Your followers should do the same. You can associate with strangers only to benefit your cause in some way.

People have to believe in your ideology to the point where they can justify their disappointment. You must involve your group members in various activities related to their interests. Don't give them the time or energy to think about your lifestyle. Use the psychology of pawns with them. These people must feel unable to escape a force they believe is greater than themselves. The way they handle the situation is by adaptation. They learn to anticipate organizational problems and cope with situations. These people, when they have been in their organization for a long time, if for some reason they realize they have made a mistake or feel they are going to be fired or ostracized, they can suddenly become very loyal. They market themselves and become your trusted friend.

3. Manipulation Through Purity

Everything is black or white. You must define what is good or bad for you. Only those thoughts, feelings, and actions that conform to your ideology are considered good. Sticking to your conscience is unreliable. Insist that kindness is achievable and that anything done in the name of kindness is ethical. Defining and manipulating the standards of good, waging total war against evil (especially dissent). Your organization must create a narrow world of guilt and shame. This must continue in the spirit of ongoing reform and the demands of a long, suffering-filled struggle to achieve goals.

Remember that, in these cases, people will be humiliated, ostracized, and punished if they do not follow your guidelines, and you must keep them in a state of guilt. Make it clear that you and the organization are the final judges of right and wrong, and use that blame and punishment to manipulate or control. Turn the environment into an unchecked authority in the eyes of others and make it clear that your power is more evident than your ability to forget.

Proclaim that everything bad comes from outside (from the world) and warn that it is best to condemn everything with great hostility. To control guilt, occasionally, you must carry out purges of heresy, mass hostilities, and jihad. You must point out the faults of all other belief systems while promoting your goodness. The impression is that you and your ways are clean, perfect, and pure.

4. The Cult of Confession

This must be closely related to the need for goodness. Confession must transcend normal religious, legal, or therapeutic expressions to the point that they become a cult in themselves. In their hands, repentance must have the meaning of exploitation, not relief from deficiencies. Confession with the leader must be an act of surrender, an expression of the individual's immersion in his ideology and system. It must dissolve the importance of ego, talent, and money. The penitential cult does not seek to subtract personal secrets but to increase and strengthen them.

5. Sacred Science

Your truth is the absolute truth. It is divine, and there is no doubt about it. You have all the answers. Only you can receive the revelation of truth. Ask them to respect you. Your moral perspective is fundamental, and anyone who dares to criticize or even wants to say anything, however small, is immoral and disrespectful. This gives members a sense of security. They trust you to answer even the most difficult questions or issues.

6. Loaded Language

Ideas end in clichés. Condense every thought into a short, very short, strong sentence easy to remember and express. Establish good terms to represent the group's ideology and demonize terms representing everything that should be rejected. Use divisive language, accompanied by jargon and exaggerated judgments; it is a language without thought. Remember, this effectively isolates the individual from the outside world and greatly limits their ability to think and feel. This loaded language gives people a sense of security.

7. Doctrine Over the Person

Doctrine replaces experience. Bring out the myth of ideology with your truth. This must replace reality. Change the story, rewrite it, or ignore it to align with your reality. Ask the individual to conform to the strict contours of your doctrinal model rather than developing your personality. Emphasizing your teaching, including its mythological element, is ultimately more valid than any experience. It requires absolute sincerity from the team. Repress emotions so that members are always happy and enthusiastic. It clarifies that all evil results from a lack of faith and evidence of wrongdoing. Consulting with others on these issues is also a sign of a lack of trust.

8. The Conflict of Existence

Who deserves to live? You have the right to decide who is worthy of living and who is not. You decide which history books are appropriate. Your followers are worth living, and others are worth dying for. Let outsiders only live when they change and enter the organization. Allow members to live in fear of being declared dead; make them fear destruction or extinction. Let them experience the emotional conflict between existence and nothingness. Make your followers' existence dependent on belief (I believe; therefore, I am), mission (I obey; therefore, I am), and more on total commitment to the organization. If they deviate from the truth, cancel existence and declare themselves dead.

Summary: These eight points are obvious and will make you a good controller. **Remember:** They can be business, political, military, guerrilla, terrorist, religious, etc. Many organizations use these strategies to transform people and generate a change in mindset.

Be vigilant, especially if they are intelligent and idealistic. Many of these people may belong to this behavioral system. This usually happens when someone says: I'm not going to get caught, this will never happen to me, I'm too smart for this kind of thing. Any resemblance to our national reality is pure coincidence.

How to Argue to Convince

It is always important to know the best way to argue. It is the dream of every advertisement to persuade. It is also the dream of politicians, negotiators, and pretenders.

Everyone deliberately tries to convince someone to believe something at some point in their lives.

There are many techniques, guides, and plans to influence people's will. Here I will leave you with the most common ways to achieve success. I will also give you some of the traps we have unknowingly entangled ourselves.

Are these ways to convince originally? Not at all. Some of these arguing methods I'm going to describe are over 2,000 years old and still valid. Moreover, anyone reading this for their amusement will discover how your politicians use every formula I am about to lay out. Campaigning is tedious when all the persuasive canons are used to scrape votes. These technologies were the first weapons to be used.

They are also widely used by various speakers and, of course, by the most stubborn of persuaders: the army of ads that hound us every day.

And do they work? These technologies are "technical." They are effective in any situation and always depend on the skill of the persuader and the target audience; otherwise, how could it be possible.

Persuasion is a skill and it is trained. Therefore, spending time on these elements cannot be considered a waste of time but a real investment.

The Use of Anticipatory Refutation

- "We have to do this, that, and the other."
- "You will wonder why we have not taken into account that."
- "Well, I'll tell you that this time we didn't consider it because of this, that, and the other."

It is a matter of presenting an argument that suits you as the sender. At the same time, you have to be aware of the objections that the addressee is likely to raise. Then you respond to these objections to prevent them from planning for you.

It is widely used in interviews and speeches to persuade audiences.

If the interviewer is skilled, they can easily dismantle the speech; if the speaker is ill-prepared or has already completed the paper written for them by their consultant, the small "yes, but..." would have dismantled the entire argument for them.

The Diagnostic Plan Approach

- Suddenly, something happens that you don't like, so you explain the nature of the problem in a more or less biased way.
- What is causing all this? Then in this part, you point out the culprit or the causes you have to fight against.
- What should be done about it? In this part, the solution is proposed as a single solution or as an ambiguous generalization to widen the room for maneuver.

- What is to be done? It proceeds to explain as if they were the only possible words.

It is supposed to be similar to the previous one. The speaker asks questions beforehand, trying to cover the whole topic, and the receiver has nothing to add. This is why the speaker did not choose to have the receiver ask.

This is an argument used a lot in interviews and electoral behavior in a very repetitive way. In electoral events, no one will respond, and beyond persuading the results, presenting the plan is a rhetorical exercise.

It works well when the audience is uncritical or uninformed. But, most importantly, benefit from the recipient's reservoir of trust when the speaker begins. Otherwise, it could be the start of a heated debate.

The Dialectic Method

You can opt to hire X services, and this has some obvious advantages that will suit you very well.

The other thing you could do is not hire anyone and take advantage of your resources, which has some big advantages and some disadvantages.

It is believed that the best option is to drop the line, which forces you to spend resources on it, and you have to reinforce more, which will end up being more productive in the long run.

The three elements of the Hegelian dialectical triad (thesis, antithesis, and synthesis) are used here, albeit on another, less esoteric level. We see much in the reasons for making difficult decisions and for taking unpopular measures.

Seen from behind and with the exact opposite reasoning, it helps justify a premeditated choice that suits us, and we strive to show that it does not pose the thesis or the antithesis.

It is not a matter of adding pros and cons to make a decision, neither more nor less; this approach is more ambitious. The course of action must be justified by acceptable and defensible reasons with this approach. On the other hand, another treatment is revealed based on other acceptable and defensible reasons. In conclusion, we propose an option, which may be intermediate or not, in which a third way out is chosen, which is a combination of the other two, or in other cases, it is the best one we propose. The logic chooses the possible exit.

The Discard Method

- "There is a problem."
- "We could do this, that, or the other."
- "It is not good for us to do this for these reasons. Nor it is good to do this for such reasons we cannot do that because then it would happen."
- "We only have the option of..."

We started with an analysis of the options, which we discarded for whatever reason. In the end, we are left with the best option or the least bad option. This is a very simple way of presenting the best options for us, best disguised as rigorous analysis. It can justify decisions that have been made in advance. It is widely used by those who have a specific advantage over the audience and are given a certain authority or expert role.

Sequential Problem Analysis

- "I have noticed that in the last few months, it has happened that..."
- "The problem is none other than..."

- "It could be easily solved if given X, but we can't, for such a reason that and that."
- "The perfect solution would be such, but it has these obstacles. Another solution is that... but it also has these conflicts, my proposal is that... which is good because of this, that and the other."
- "In case you accept my solution, I propose that we do the following..."

This is a logical and reasonable way. But it is full of pitfalls. It assumes that someone states the facts objectively. Then, you diagnose the nature of the problem. Next, you describe the obstacles encountered in solving the problem. There are always obstacles detected by experts, legal, logistical, economic, etc. Finally, possible solutions and their advantages and disadvantages are presented. These solutions are material discarded by the viewers. Then, comes the convenient options and how to proceed.

A Simple Plan for Convincing

- "This just happened..."
- "Which leads to this cause..."
- "Then what remains for us to do is..."

For less demanding contexts, the above approach can be simplified. In this case, we don't try so hard to detail the problem. Instead, we discuss how it got here and what the solution was. This is for less demanding audiences and all kinds of obvious dilemmas where decisions need to be made.
It is effective when there is little margin (of time or resources) or when the public is not critical or does not participate.

The Solutions Method

- "I notice that you need to cover the lack of a good..."
- "I do not understand why they have held out for so long, because there are good solutions, like this one I am showing you; they are solutions that..."
- "I already realize that the best solution that there is besides the fact that it is on sale is that..."

This is a very crude method used in sales, but useful. It is similar to the previous one but bypasses the diagnostic stage and goes straight to the solution stage. It is based on the fact that there is a need, but there is no reason why it exists or if anything can be done to avoid it. Then provide several solutions in the "table of contents," each with its advantages. In the end, you decide on the most feasible solution for the audience based on their reactions or any previous research done before the presentation.

This is a very simple approach, but it is not ineffective if the audience finds their key moments well chosen.

For example, if you offer a new security system, by showing it after they have suddenly had a DDoS-type problem, you can show them how they will be more secure now.

Improvement Solutions

- "There is a situation that is not going very well or is working, but it could be better."
- "If we do X, then we would achieve many advantages."
- "When we achieve these advantages, what could be done is that we improve all this..."

- "So, step by step, over time, we can modernize this system, solve this vulnerability in the current situation, and we will achieve to be better."

In all forms of argumentation, it is a very useful method when you cannot or do not want to make significant changes in situations that clearly can be improved. In this case, incremental, slow improvements are used until the situation changes.

Some would say that this is tinkering with something that doesn't work; in fact, it usually is. The point is that we can't always make fundamental changes. Think about real tax reform in a country or pension reform. On a smaller scale, we can imagine what it means to change a company's entire compensation system suddenly.

Counterarguments

- "According to the government, doing X thing will achieve Y, but the government doesn't count that... neither that... nor this, nor that..."
- "Therefore, what should be done is... because we would achieve such and such... this... that... the other..."

It assumes that opposing arguments are revealed in a more or less biased way and articulated by extracting problems from the preceding argument. Then, our position is stated without any problem.

It is widely used in prepared interviews where someone will present an idea for their previous work. This is a very popular form of political exposition.

It is often used when the counterpart is not present to refute detected negative aspects that are often not so negative or have an exaggerated nature or significance.

A Classic Convincing Method

For the nostalgic or curious, I have included a summary of the original approach with the argumentative form of the classical orator. In this way, the oldest debates of the early democracies have been elaborated, and the most influential speeches succeeded in persuading audiences to justify war, siege, and great human change.

The method is very simple and involves the following 5 rigorous steps. This is a characteristic, rigidity, which is very prominent in ancient speech.

1 *Invention* or the choice of arguments.

2 *Disposition* or the organization of an expository plan of which you will speak later.

3 *Elocution* or the arrangement of language to make a better impression.

4 **Memory**. It is possible to read the speech, but this is not an option because it would have disabled the speaker's credibility.

5 *Pronunciation* or exposition is loaded with verbal inflections, emotionality, theatricality, and more.

The plan itself is organized in 4 phases, which are always rigid and permanent.

1 The exordium or the call for attention and the statement of the problem and what is going to be dealt with.

2 The narration is where the facts, pros, and cons are exposed.

3   The recapitulation with the summary of the ideas transmitted or the conclusions reached.

4   The peroration or emotional phase is where the audience is mobilized to take action.

Some inspiration may have come from the classical approach, but honestly, if Aristotle spoke in one of our auditoriums, the public would be perplexed by the performance, and Aristotle himself would have to leave by the back door.

There are many ways to persuade individuals or groups. Certainly, all of these speech exercises can be trained and improved. However, less obvious, and what almost everyone forgets, is that we are subjective at heart, which leads us into our argumentative traps and locks us into recurring stubbornness in our interpersonal strategies.

Chapter 6: Brainwashing

Brainwashing takes us one level beyond the mind control we addressed in the previous chapter. In this chapter, I want to show you how people have been brainwashed, what happens when they are brainwashed, and the roots of this strategy that is practically landing in the Deep Web of manipulation.

We will learn what it is, who has used it, and the different types of brainwashing done, from the Asians against the Americans to the present day.

What Is Brainwashing?

Several movies tell us about brainwashing, such as those showing how the Vietnamese communists brainwashed American soldiers. However, far from the dramatization of these movies, brainwashing, better understood if we call it coercive persuasion, includes influence and compulsion. This type of persuasion is the most persuasive and aggressive and is usually carried out by sects, totalitarian states, terrorist groups, and kidnappers.

Brainwashing a person, or more precisely, coercive persuasion is not easy. For a person to change his entire belief system, the way people think, feel, and behave, several techniques must be used. These coercive persuasion techniques can be divided into 4 types: environment-based, emotion-based, cognition-based, and dissociative state induction techniques.

I will show them in a theoretical way.

1. Environmental Brainwashing

This type of technology intervenes in an object by controlling or manipulating its environment. Their task is to weaken resistance to facilitate persuasion. **Some contextual techniques of coercive persuasion are the following:**

- **Isolation:** It works to give effectiveness to persuasion. It is about encapsulating the subject from the psychic, social, and physical world. In other words, total isolation.

- **Information control:** The control and manipulation of information is a way of isolation. With less information, the consequence will be less choice and less critical thinking.

- **Establishing a state of existential dependency:** This consists of making one person's existence dependent on another, usually a leader. Its practice includes satisfying primary and secondary needs until total dependence arises.

- **Psychophysiological weakening:** Physical weakening is related to psychological weakening, leading to a reduced capacity to resist persuasion techniques.

Since it is about the superfluous, propaganda, persuasion, and marketing mechanisms are used to induce others to consume something and make them believe that the superficial is necessary and that there is a secret source of happiness.

2. Emotional Techniques

Emotions condition motivations. If emotions can be influenced, they can influence motivation and, at the same time, behavior. **Here are 2 techniques for forcing emotional persuasion:**

- **Activate the emotion of joy:** this is about moving with liking. It is used to attract people, and gain followers.
- **Emotional activation of fear, guilt, and anxiety:** through the use of rewards and punishments, emotional responses of fear, guilt, and anxiety are established. Emotions encourage dependence and submission.

3. Cognitive Techniques

Previous techniques mediate this type of coercive persuasion technique. A theme of fragility and guilt is perfect for cognitive persuasion. **Some of these techniques are described below:**

- **Denigration of critical thinking:** This is about showing the invalidity of following thoughts. Every time they suffer, they are repressed or denigrated.
- **Using lies and deception:** This is about distorting reality and information by hiding, lying, or deceiving.
- **Demand for condescendence:** It is to establish group thinking or to conform to what the group decides, is another strategy. It is to create a habit of conformity and submission.
- **Identification with the group:** Identification must be collected so that each individual loses their individuality and accepts the

group's individuality. This pressure can depersonalize individuals, losing the identity factors that distinguish them.

- **Attention control:** Manipulates the presentation of stimuli and controls attention to the points of persuasion.
- **Controlling language:** controls language and reduces freedom. For example, words are suppressed, and some questions or valuations are avoided.
- **Change of power source:** Once all one's power principles are overthrown, all power is exposed. This authority figure gathers all powers and the others obey them.

People can deal with each other in only 2 ways, logic or arms. Persuasion or force. Those who know they cannot win with logic always end up taking the gun.

4. Dissociative State Induction Techniques

Dissociation corresponds to the trance-like state that results from the intensification of experience. These states result in a temporary loss of consciousness and identity and are more likely to occur in totalitarian environments. In addition, these states of consciousness make followers more vulnerable, so they can be guided by limiting their possible options and reducing their ability to evaluate them.

In short, coercive persuasion, also known as "brainwashing," consists of manipulating the environment to weaken the subject. From there, cognitive and emotional persuasion will change the way you think and feel and ultimately lead you into a more persuasive trance.

How is this technique carried out? The term "brainwashing" was coined by journalist Edward Hunt during the Korean War to describe a technique used by the Chinese to "re-educate" American prisoners.

In the broadest interpretation of the word, brainwashing is associated with cults and often uses combined psychological methods to make its followers obey its slogans.

Chanting mantras is an important feature of many religions, especially Buddhism and Hinduism, and almost all churches, have some form of hymn worship.

The combined voices of all choir members bring a strong sense of unity and identity to the group. However, the constant repetition of short tones is designed to eliminate logical thinking and lead to a trance-like state.

Other Techniques and Examples

Isolation

In 1977, Jim Jones and about 1,000 members of his religious group, the People's Temple, moved to an isolated commune in Guyana. Some 400 kilometers of jungle separated them from the U.S. embassy in Guyana's capital, Georgetown. This isolation helped the sect members lose their values to the outside world, which allowed Jones to inculcate the teachings of his terrible regime.

Far from the influence and cruel punishment of their friends and family in the United States, the members of the People's Temple had no choice but to obey Jones. In terms of total control and forced isolation of its members, the People's Temple's "agricultural" project is often compared to countries like North Korea or Albania before 1991.

Dependency and Fear

Patty Hearst, the heiress to the media empire her grandfather William Randolph Hearst founded in 1974, was kidnapped by a small leftist group called the Symbiosis Liberation Army, a classic example of brainwashing through dependency and fear.

Physical and sexual abuse quickly turned Hearst from a young socialite into a member of this terrorist group that even robbed banks.

After her arrest, Hearst was locked in a closet and subjected to physical and sexual abuse. As a result, the terrorists had total control over her life. This dependence on captives leads to what is known as "Stockholm Syndrome."

Shortly after that, on April 5th, 1974, Hearst was photographed with an assault rifle while robbing the Hibernia Bank.

Pedagogical Activity

How does the teacher encourage his students to behave and obey? The answer usually involves incorporating some form of physical activity or sport.

Focus on jumping and running so that, physically tired, students are less likely to argue or create problems. Aware of this phenomenon, several cults seek to occupy members through strenuous meetings as a means of control.

Lack of Sleep and Fatigue

Sensory overload, disorientation, and lack of sleep can alter our ability to make good decisions.

This fatigue-based technique, combined with sleep deprivation, is based on instructing cult members to follow a special diet containing small amounts of protein and other important nutrients. Thus, cult members are always tired and unable to resist the domination of the ideology.

Self-Criticism and Finger-Pointing

During the Korean War of 1950-1952, imprisoned American soldiers were subjected to so-called "self-criticism" by the Chinese, who had to condemn their comrades, talk about their mistakes, and express criticism of capitalism.

At first, the POWs regarded these meetings as "naive." Later, however, this process of "criticism" led to real doubts about the effectiveness of their country and the war.

Despite some limited success, this approach has generally not been successful. Nevertheless, the Maoist Chinese government uses it throughout the country.

Love Bombing

Cults try to create the impression that the world outside the group is hostile and wrong. To highlight the contrast, the "love bombing" technique is often used. This method shows maximum affection and concern for new or potential recruits.

It is common sense in social psychology: we have a strong tendency to return the kindness and generosity of others.

Mystical Manipulation

Many cults rely on mysterious manipulations to gain total control over their followers. This refers to the control of the environment or information by cult leaders to convey the impression of supernatural intelligence, divine grace, or magical power.

In other words, the cult leader presents himself as a trusted messenger of God, is always right, and backs it up with impressive tricks.

You must understand that those who try to brainwash others tend to prey on the weak and vulnerable. Of course, not all people are targets for mind control. But, at different times, some people have more susceptibility to some control modes. A skilled manipulator knows what to look for and targets people going through difficult times in their lives or changes that may or may not be voluntary.

The list of possible candidates includes:

- People who become unemployed are fearful about the future.
- Recently divorced people, especially if it was a bitter divorce.
- Those going through long illnesses, especially when it is an illness they do not understand.
- Those who lost a loved one, especially if they were close to the person and have few friends.
- Young people who are away from home for the first time are the favorites of religious sect leaders.
- A specific predatory tactic is for you to find out information about the person and the belief system so that you explain the tragedy they are experiencing in a way that is consistent with the belief system. This can then explain the overall story through that belief system while subtly modifying itself according to the manipulator's interpretation.

You should be wary of people who try to isolate you or a person you know has outside influences, such as those who experience a tragedy in their life or some major change and feel alone. Manipulators work on increasing feelings of loneliness and isolation that can take many forms.

- In the case of young people who fall into a cult, they are likely to avoid contact with friends and family members.
- In the case of a partner in an abusive relationship, they may never cease to be the victim and may be kept out of sight of the abused or not allowed contact with friends and family.
- In the case of prisoners in an enemy prison camp, it may involve isolating them from each other while they are subjected to overt or subtle torture.

It attacks the victim's self-esteem. Brainwashing occurs only when the manipulator is in a position of superiority over the victim. This means the victim's self-esteem must be destroyed for the manipulator to rebuild it in his or her image and likeness. It can be done by mental, emotional, or physical means for as long as it takes to wear the victim down physically and emotionally.

- Mental torture can begin with a lie to the victim and can be given more and more until it intimidates or embarrasses the victim. This form of torture occurs with words or gestures ranging from expressions of disapproval to invading the victim's personal space.
- Emotional torture does not have kindness, of course, but starts with insults and moves on to harassment, spitting, or dehumanizing things like stripping the victim naked to have his or her picture taken or just to be seen.

- Physical torture can include starvation, freezing, not being allowed to sleep, beatings, mutilation, and other acts that are not accepted by society. Physical torture is often used by abusive parents and partners and is also used in prisons and re-education camps.

You should pay attention to people who seek to be part of a more attractive group than the outside world. Along with the undermining of resistance, it is good if the victim is provided with an alternative, apparently more attractive looking than what they knew before connecting with that manipulator.

This can be done in various ways:

- Only those who are already brainwashed are allowed contact with others, thus creating a peer pressure mode that encourages the victim to want to look like the new group members and seek acceptance. This can be reinforced through contact, small talk, group sex, or stricter means such as a dress code, a controlled diet, and other means.
- Repeat the message by means ranging from chanting the same phrase many times to emphasizing keywords or phrases.
- Mimic the rhythm of the human heartbeat through the leader's speech or music cadence. This can be augmented with lighting that is neither too dim nor too bright, with a good temperature that relaxes the person.
- Do not let the victim have time to think. This may be because they are never going to stop being bombarded with constant content on topics beyond their comprehension and at the same time the refusal to answer their questions.

- An us-versus-them mentality must be presented, where the leader is right, and everyone else is wrong. The goal is for blind obedience to be achieved whereby the victim surrenders money and life to the manipulator and the stated goals.

Related to this topic is hypnosis, which also achieves control but in a more intense way. In the next chapter, I will tell you about it to understand how far manipulation goes through dark psychology.

Chapter 7: Hypnosis

First, you need to consider being clear about hypnosis to better protect yourself from unethical use. Below you will discover the specific ways in which cults and sects use mind control hypnosis to manipulate their members and how to use it yourself if you so desire.

What Is Hypnosis?

Many people would think of oscillating clocks on stage and hypnotists making people do weird things like cluck as chickens!

It is more useful to think of hypnosis in terms of states of consciousness. Everyone has a waking state in which they know they are awake, aware, alert, alive, and in the world. In addition, we have different stages of consciousness throughout the day. For example, if you take a hot shower and feel a little drowsy, your mind may have begun to divagate, lazily shifting from one thought to another. This is an altered state of consciousness or trance state. Another example is staring at fish movement in a large fish tank. What happens is that your attention becomes more and more focused, and your awareness of your surroundings decreases.

This is a classic hypnotic state in which attention is shifted to what is happening inside rather than what is happening outside. You become more aware of your thoughts, inner image, and feelings and less aware of what is going on in your environment. This is usually very pleasant, relaxing, and pleasurable for most people.

An important factor here is that trance states impair the ability to think logically and critically. As a result, you tend to accept any information given regardless of whether it is reasonable or unreasonable. This means that a person under hypnosis is susceptible to suggestion and uncritically accepts any suggestion given. This means that even people with strong personalities can be hypnotized and do things they would not normally do. Rational analysis, conscious decision-making, and judgment are suspended; this is a reward for cult leaders. After all, they don't want members to think for themselves!

Think of mind control hypnosis plus all the mind control techniques and strategies I have been telling you about. They have a very powerful set of tools to manipulate others and even manipulate them to do things that go against their ethics and moral principles.

Interestingly, many cult leaders often claim that people cannot do things against their will, even with mind control hypnosis. There are two major issues with this:

First, group members are programmed to accept what the leader has to say. They will simply tend to accept the idea. Second, the implicit idea is that if the person does something, they do it of their own free will. When we make our own decisions, we believe more strongly and are more committed to them, and the results, actions, and effects of our choices last longer. It's a subtle but very powerful idea.

Another thing to keep in mind is that hypnosis is not always a process of closing your eyes. You don't have to close your eyes to enter a trance state. For example, have you ever driven, but don't remember much of the trip when you arrive at your destination? You're in a daze! People often drive in a trance state with their eyes wide open, working! If they see someone pull out before them, it's not hard to stop and take the necessary steps to avoid an accident.

People often have the idea that there are special hypnotic words that can induce trance. Hypnosis can be triggered in seemingly normal conversations, using everyday language without even saying "relax," "deep," or "sleep." But that is another matter.

Hypnosis can even be induced without words. For example, if you have a massage, the therapist doesn't have to speak, just rub your muscles and manipulate your limbs, allowing you to relax more and more and focus inward.

Other Hypnosis Occur Naturally

When people are bored or tired, they often find that their attention is turned inward, outward, and away from the outside world. Also, it is often easier to hypnotize a person in this state. Especially an unscrupulous hypnotist or cult leader would use this natural hypnosis to implant signals in people. Remember, the advice to use mind control hypnosis in cults and sects is for the leader's benefit!

Peer pressure is another powerful force that pushes people into trance states. If everyone around you is doing the same thing, it can be very difficult not to follow the team, especially when the team leader berates everyone for being different!

Keep in mind these important points about hypnosis:

- Hypnosis is just an altered state.
- You naturally enter many altered states or trances on your own every day.
- You do not have to have your eyes closed.
- Hypnosis can be induced without words, and most importantly, it reduces critical thinking faculties and the ability to evaluate information.

When hypnosis is carried out for a long time, it can lead to brainwashing, which is the slow process of taking a victim's ideas, looking at their identity and beliefs, and then changing them to new ideas that will suit the manipulator's purpose; this process can occur in a broad and narrow context. For example, the brainwasher could use techniques to gain control of the person, or they could use techniques to control the mind of a larger group at the same time.

The brainwashing process is the starting point where social circumstances and the victim's mental state are taken. It is the basis for the rest of the process; if the manipulator cannot resolve this, the brainwashing session will not succeed. Brainwashing is not a process that works for everyone. It requires a good identification that is looking for something or a person who has a void they are trying to fill.

All this brings us to an important point, who is the ideal victim of brainwashing, people who have had their reality shaken by recent events are the best targets for brainwashing. If they lost a person they were very close to, or because of a dramatic event in their life, then they may be more susceptible to brainwashing. The brainwashing process begins when the brainwasher finds the victim, either through the internet or in person. Contrary to the popular image that may be held in mind about brainwashing, it will often look like a rational, friendly, and calm person.

The person who has life seems to be able to give their own to the other person. Imagine feeling helpless and that a celebrity you admired has become a friend, usually, this is what the process of encountering brainwashing by the victim feels like.

The brainwashing begins to work. The first step is to generate a level of trust and rapport between them and the victim. This is done with superficial similarities and deep relationships. The superficial similarities involve some surface-level preferences, like enjoying the same food or sport as the other person.

Then, you move to a deeper level of relationship; some of these may involve the deepest shared experience you have had in the past. Surely, the brainwasher fakes them convincingly to create the bonds, so if the victim shares with the brainwasher that they lost a close relative, suddenly the brainwasher has a similar story to share with the victim.

The false connection and emotional warmth are not the only things that will happen, and the brainwasher wants to connect that link as fast as possible. It is not uncommon to give presents and favors to the victim. You can send a gadget, or anything technological when it is useful to them. You can invite him or her to lunch. The goal is to create a sense of gratitude and indebtedness to the person, which will soften a lot of the victim's resistance.

After the resistance has been removed somewhat, the other step is a sort of utopian presentation. This will involve brainwashing slowly and incrementally, offering a solution to any and every problem the victim has ever had. This is not going to be a big push or sell. On the contrary, the brainwasher knows how to do this casually to make sure they don't deal with negatives by putting pressure on the victim. The solution will always be the personality, ideology, or cult that the mind washer works to make the victim become.

When these steps are done correctly, the initial stages of our discussion will leave victims wanting more. Victims will want more information and a greater understanding of the solutions suggested by the brainwasher. The brainwasher may even withhold some of this information at first, treating it as something the victim needs to work to achieve. The purpose of this is to motivate victims to seek out and accept the message they will eventually hear. Brainwashers are careful to reveal the right information at the right time after the victims have been indoctrinated as part of this belief system for some time and have demonstrated that they will respond well to it. This is a concept called "progressive disclosure" or "milk before meat." It will consist of coming up with an accessible idea before the controversial point is discovered.

For example, if brainwashers try to turn victims into religious terrorists, they do not simply start with the terrorism part. Instead, they may initially begin by focusing on God's love for the victim, which the person can accept. The more objectionable thoughts, such as those God wants you to analyze, are the ones that stick around until later in the process. Once the victim accepts the last part, there is no turning back from this brainwashing process. At this point, you may wonder why victims are still engaging in brainwashing, especially when these more objectionable thoughts begin to become evident. There are some reasons:

Brainwashing works easier on vulnerable victims. They have a strong sense that they love being manipulated and want recognition; that is why they respond well to hypnosis. By now, victims have invested some time and, in some cases, money in the process. This is often referred to as the irrecoverable cost fallacy. Victims will feel it is a bad idea to waste all the hard work and money they invested in the process. The hypnotist has been accumulating large amounts of sensitive and secret information about the target. They are often willing to keep this information about their victims to keep them on the right track.

Hypnosis, Control, and Manipulation in Environments Like Cults and Organizations

I would like to talk to you about the negative uses of hypnosis that employ mind control as their goal, especially when it is done with bad intentions.

The realm of control must always belong to the individual, that is, to you. For instance, using hypnosis to get a person to quit smoking is excellent as long as the hypnotist allows the desire and control to quit smoking to be in the client's hands, rather than trying to transfer it to himself. Today, many mind control techniques are much more sophisticated than those approaches used in World War II and the Korean War. Some include covert forms of hypnosis, while others are implemented through social environments and very strict and controlled destructive cults. Most importantly, remember that mind control is a very delicate process. All destructive cults use mind control techniques and hypnosis.

Although I do not want to focus on the topic of sects, it is valid to mention that they are not something new. Throughout history, many groups of enthusiasts have rallied around charismatic leaders of all kinds. However, in recent times, leaders have begun to use psychological tools such as hypnosis to subjugate the will of a person and achieve control of their thoughts, behavior, and feelings.

Similarly, we cannot leave out another technique that began to affect the public: the use of NLP, which, combined with hypnosis, mind control, and brainwashing, get more people to adopt a certain type of thought or behavior.

Initially, these methods were only available to volunteer participants and there were many positive experiences. Soon, however, some of these techniques permeated the general culture of popular psychology and could easily be misused by anyone. Unscrupulous people began to practice them for money and power, manipulating whoever they wanted, not only in cults but also one person who manipulated another, be it employees, friends, partners...

Mind control practiced by destructive people and cults is a social process, often associated with large numbers of followers who reinforce it. This is done by placing the individual in a social environment in which, for them to be accepted, they must forsake their old identity and cling to the new one required by the group. Any reality that might remind him or her of their old identity, anything that might confirm their old selves, is pushed aside and replaced by the group reality. Even if at first the individual only pretends to accept it, sooner or later this behavior will become reality. He or she embraced a totalitarian ideology that, when internalized, replaced their previous value system. Typically, people undergo a fundamental change in personality and experience a dramatic interruption in the course of their lives. This process can be activated in a few hours, but it usually takes days or weeks to be internalized. It happens in sects, with individuals, in political groups, etc.

Of course, all of us are affected by various social pressures every day, and this is most evident in our work. The pressure to accept certain norms of behavior is present in almost all organizations. We are often influenced in many ways, some of which are obvious (e.g., signs of "Please fasten your seat belt"), while others are more subtle and destructive. In this sense, I can't say for sure that when I use the term "mind control" I'm specifically referring to the destructive end of the spectrum. Therefore, as I have previously emphasized, the term "mind control" does not apply to certain techniques, for example, biofeedback, which is used to enhance personal control and stimulus selection, an excellent strategy. Instead, I am referring only to systems that seek to undermine an individual's ability to make their decisions. In this case, control with hypnosis encourages dependency and conformity and discourages autonomy and individuality.

If the term "brainwashing" is often confused with "mind control", the term "hypnosis" is also often misunderstood. Using the word "hypnotize" in various forms is very common in our daily conversations (we often say things like "she hypnotized him with her smile"). Most people don't understand what hypnosis is about. When listening to the word, the first image that comes to our mind is of a bearded doctor swinging an old pocket watch or a bracelet in front of a man with closed eyelids. While the image is certainly a stereotype, it points to the central goal of hypnosis: trance. The hypnotized person enters a trance state that is fundamentally different from normal consciousness. The difference is that in a normal state of consciousness, attention is directed outward through the five senses, whereas, in a trance state, attention is directed inward. A person hears, sees, and feels inside. Naturally, there are various degrees of trance, from the mild trance state of normal dreaming to the deep state in which the individual is almost completely ignorant of the outside world and extremely vulnerable to the suggestions at play that may be implanted in his or her mind. Hypnosis has been linked in many ways to the unethical mind control practices of destructive cults. In many sects that define themselves as religions, what is commonly called "meditation" is nothing more than the process by which its members enter a state of trance, a time in which they can receive advice that facilitates them following the teachings of the sect. Secular denominations present individuals or groups in other ways. Also, since being in a trance is usually a joyful experience, most people want to go back into this sate as much as possible. In particular, psychological researchers have clinically shown that an individual's critical abilities are diminished in a trance state. A person is less able to evaluate the information received in a trance state than in a normal state of consciousness.

The ability of hypnosis to affect people is considerable. They can go into a trance state for a few minutes and then perform extraordinary feats. Perhaps the most famous example is when the hypnotized subject uses a long needle in the thigh and feels no pain. A hypnotized person may dance like Michael Jackson, lie as rigid as a stiff board between two chairs, act as if his hands were "glued" to his sides, etc. If they can be forced to accomplish such a feat, it is also easy to convince the hypnotized subject that they are part of a "minority." Destructive cults often send their members into a trance state through lengthy indoctrination sessions. Repetition and forced attention are great ways to induce a trance state. If we observe a group in that stage, it is easy to distinguish when a trance state is reached. Those people under this condition blink, swallow slowly, and their facial expressions are relaxed into a blank, neutral behavior. For people in this state, unscrupulous leaders can implant irrational beliefs. I have seen some very strong-willed people who get hypnotized and do things that they normally would never do.

That's how invasive hypnosis can be and you should be careful not only of sects, organizations, or politicians but also of closer dangers, those that can hypnotize you even in your own home.

Chapter 8: Emotional Intelligence

Emotional intelligence is the ability to identify, understand, and adequately manage reactions to facilitate relationships with others, achieve goals and objectives, stress management, or overcome obstacles.

Positive and negative emotions will be there in the face of any life event. Depending on your ability to cope with them, they can help you, make you happy, or plunge you into absolute misery.

Emotionally intelligent people do not necessarily have fewer negative emotions, but they know how to handle them better when they arise. They also have a greater ability to identify themselves and know exactly how they feel, and they also have a high ability to identify how others feel. By recognizing and understanding emotions better, they can use them to relate better to others (empathy), be more successful at work, and lead more fulfilling lives.

In 1995, Daniel Goleman published his book *Emotional Intelligence*, but little did he know it would soon become a worldwide bestseller. The analysis of new emotional dimensions has attracted the attention of people eager to know and learn more about themselves.

In his publication, the American psychologist argues that a person's success depends not only on their IQ or academic research but also on emotional knowledge. When we talk about emotional intelligence, we refer to an individual's ability to identify their emotional state and manage it properly. This ability has a very positive effect on those who possess it, as it allows them to understand and control their impulses and facilitates communicative relationships with others.

Benefits of Emotional Intelligence

Related to the above, the development of emotional intelligence should be considered to manage emotions and make them beneficial to the actions and decisions taken. Goleman defines emotional intelligence as the ability to cope with setbacks, control impulses and delay gratification, regulate emotions and empathize with others. Emotional intelligence is divided into five components:

1   Self-awareness
2   Self-motivation
3   Self-regulation
4   Empathy
5   Social skills

How much time do you spend with yourself and your emotions? Many times, you can spend time with everything around you except yourself. Your people are the greatest resource you have, and many things depend on you, so it is necessary to understand the benefits you will get if you take the time to work on your emotional intelligence.

Here are some benefits that will surely help you in your daily work:

- **Improves decision making:** It allows people to assess their value and belief systems, helps identify strengths and weaknesses to improve, and is necessary to make better decisions in life.
- **Improves work performance:** Emotional intelligence applied to work can be very useful in different ways. For example, it

increases employee productivity, improves occupational health, customer service, etc.

- **Protects against and avoids stress:** Proper emotional management is as important to protect against stress as avoiding stress itself. Imagine any situation where a lack of empathy and poor emotional regulation can lead to ongoing arguments and increased personal worry. All of this creates a stressful environment for you and others in the long run.

- **Encourages personal development:** Coaches, i.e., personal development specialists, provide students with emotional intelligence tools since, without adequate self-knowledge and management of our emotions, it is impossible to understand an individual's personal development. On the other hand, poor emotional management can affect the learning process because they alter focus, concentration, memory, and motivation, resulting in a stagnation of personal growth.

- **Provides leadership capacity:** Emotional intelligence is an essential skill for leaders. A leader's emotional self-control or understanding of others is a good reflection of leadership. Indeed, many charismatic leaders, those with high emotional intelligence, such as transformational leaders, have proven to be the most efficient in many surveys because they motivate and increase the productivity and effectiveness of their teams.

- **Promotes psychological well-being:** Many current ailments are associated with proper emotional management, and as such, it is used as a treatment. Inadequate management of emotions can generate long-term anxiety due to negative appraisals of reality or inadequate sentimental control. Emotional intelligence can help prevent anxiety symptoms. A recent meta-analysis of 7,898 subjects found that high levels of emotional intelligence were significantly associated with good mental health. On the other hand, some studies have found that low levels of emotional intelligence are associated with certain emotional imbalances, such as symptoms of depression and anxiety.

- **Promotes physical health wellness:** Every day, research supports the claim that emotions and our body are interconnected and interact, triggering chemical reactions that alter the immune response and the functioning of our different organs and systems both physically and mentally. Physically, disorders of the cardiovascular system, respiratory system, musculoskeletal disorders (muscle and joint pain), gastric disorders (ulcers, colitis, irritable bowel syndrome), and immune system disorders can occur. (Ortega, 2010).

- Understandably, investing time in developing emotional intelligence can greatly impact our quality of life. Think about it now. How do you feel about your life right now? Do you think these benefits will affect your personal or work life? It is important that our life today is more balanced professionally, personally, emotionally, cognitively, and socially because many times, when we forget about the emotional aspect, the other dimensions that make up our person can be compromised little by little.

As I told you before, the acquisition of emotional intelligence implies the development of specific skills, all of which are essential for a good social adjustment. People with developed emotional skills are more likely to feel satisfied and productive in life.

Skills to Impact and Manipulate Others

There are many different types of intelligence; your job is to discover what they are and how to incorporate them into your life. Sources of intelligence can be measured by ratios. Most of us are familiar with IQ or Intelligence Quotient, which relates primarily to our ability to remember and recall items from memory and reason logically.

There is also the CQ or Curiosity Quotient, which refers to your ability to have a strong drive to learn a particular subject. Finally, the definition of emotional intelligence (first proposed by researchers Peter Salovey and John Mayer, but popularized by author Daniel Goleman) is the ability to:

In practice, it means being aware that emotions can drive your behavior and affect people (both positive and negative) and learning to manage those emotions, both your own and others, especially when under stress.

We are emotional creatures, often making decisions and responding to stimuli based on our emotions. Therefore, our ability to develop emotional intelligence greatly impacts all our relationships, how we make decisions, and spot opportunities. Therefore, emotional intelligence is very important. I have identified 10 skills that I believe characterize people with high emotional intelligence through my work.

I hope you will gain courage from these and learn to understand how to influence your mind and the minds of others, through daily emotional growth, in everything you do.

Empathy

This is the ability to understand or feel what the other person is experiencing from your frame of reference, i.e., the ability to put yourself in the other person's shoes.

There are 2 kinds of empathy:

1 "Emotional empathy" refers to the feelings and emotions you get in response to another person's emotions; this can include mirroring that person's feelings or simply feeling stressed when you discover another person's fears or anxiety.

2 "Cognitive empathy," sometimes called "empathy," refers to the ability to recognize and understand the emotions of others.

We are empathetic based on the reactions of others. I would also argue that empathy can be cultivated and learned through experience. Keep in your memory how you feel when you react and see things. Write down these thoughts, analyze them and decide how you would like to be treated by others.

Self-Awareness

Self-awareness is the art of knowing ourselves, identifying the stimuli we face, and preparing ourselves to know how to handle them proactively and reactively. Self-awareness is how we see ourselves and how we see others. The second external aspect is always the most difficult to assess correctly.

Dr. Tasha Eurich says, "Leaders who are focused on creating internal and external self-awareness, who seek honest feedback from others and ask questions of what, rather than why can learn to see themselves for themselves and reap many rewards that self-awareness offers."

Ask introspective questions, crave knowledge, be curious about others, and find feedback in spaces of affection and honesty.

Curiosity

Give me a curious person eager to learn and improve, and I'll tell you about an upcoming success story. When you are curious, you are passionate, and when you are passionate, it drives you to want to be the best. Your "antenna" depends on what you like, want to grow, and learn more. This learning mentality positively impacts other relational aspects of your life.

Tomas Chamorro-Premuzic writes, "First, people with higher CQ are generally more tolerant of ambiguity. This subtle, complex, and subtle thinking defines the nature of complexity. Second, CQ leads to higher levels of intellectual investment and knowledge acquired over time, especially in areas of formal knowledge."

Analytical Mind

The most emotionally intelligent and decisive people are deep thinkers who analyze and process all new information that comes to them. They continue to analyze information, habits, and ways of doing things to see if they can find ways to improve. We are all "analysts" because we consciously think about all the new information we encounter.

Emotional intelligence specialists are everyday problem solvers and philosophers who think about the "why" of being, the "why" of doing what we do, and are passionately concerned about living virtuous lives. Having an analytical mind means having a healthy appetite for a continuous improvement mindset that aims to improve ourselves and is always open to new ideas.

Believing

An important part of maintaining emotional self-control is harnessing the power of faith to believe in your present and future self.

Faith alone will not help you. Take action, of course. But when you combine belief with strong values like hard work, perseverance, and a positive attitude, you lay the foundation for a champion. Every great leader and thinker uses faith, whether in a practical, emotional, or, spiritual context.

Take the time to meditate. Think about how you believe in yourself. Develop greater confidence in yourself and who you want to be. Trust and believe that the parts of your life will come together to help you live a courageous and happy life.

Needs and Wants

Emotionally intelligent minds can differentiate between what they need and what they correctly classify as a need that is "nice to have." A need, especially in the context of Abraham Maslow's "hierarchy of needs," is the basic level of safety, survival, and maintenance. Once these things are met, you can move on to other needs and, of course, wants.

"Want" is a nice house, a nice car, or even a new iPhone. We don't need these things to survive, but we want them according to our desires or what we think is important to society. You must become an expert at understanding what you need in life to achieve your goals and provide for yourself and your loved ones. Make sure you make a very clear distinction between what you need and what you want.

Emotionally intelligent people know the difference between this and always establish needs before satisfying their wants.

Passion

Inspirational leadership and love for what one does stems from the passion for a subject or a person. Emotionally intelligent people use their passion and purpose to ignite the engines that drive them to do what they do. This passion is contagious: it permeates every aspect of their lives and affects those around them.

Passion is like "I don't know what it is," you know it when you feel it or see it in someone else. Passion is a natural desire, instinct, drive, ambition, and love inspired by a subject or someone. Passion brings positive energy that helps sustain us and motivates us to move forward. Emotionally intelligent and enthusiastic people are known to be willing to persevere and move forward in any situation.

Optimism

If you want to increase your chances, improve your relationships, and think clearly and constructively, you must have a positive attitude. In all the things you try to control and influence, your attitude is always in your control. Therefore, you can choose to live each day positively. It is easy.

When we are happy, when our mindset and emotions are positive, we are smarter, more motivated, and more successful. Happiness is at the core and success surrounds it.

Adaptability

Emotionally intelligent people know when to continue with their lessons and when to make changes. This important awareness and ability to make accurate and quick decisions is called adaptability. You have to decide when to stay the course and when to continue in the other direction.

Also, when one strategy doesn't work, try to evaluate and determine if other strategies will work. From the way you treat yourself, to the way you treat others, in your daily life, always be open and willing to adapt and introduce new elements into how you think and behave.

You will have to change routes throughout your life and evaluate whether you will be happy if you choose one route or another. Realize that you can always change. You can always start over. It may not always be the wisest or most prudent decision, but only you can determine what is or isn't.

Interest in Success to Others and Yourself

Finally, an emotionally intelligent person is interested in overall success and achievement, not only for themselves but also for their peers. Their inspirational leadership and enthusiasm, combined with their optimism, drive them to want to do what is best for themselves and others.

Too often, we are also focused and only worry about "what about me?" Of course, we need to worry about that. This is imperative, so don't let anyone discourage you. But just as we must focus on our interests, we must also maintain a spirit of desire and hope to see those around us succeed.

Not only is this an excellent protection against jealousy and greed, but it also rekindles our passion and propels us toward our next goal. In addition, it helps us gain allies and build strong relationships that, in turn, reciprocally help us.

Once you have managed to develop emotional intelligence, you have to work in various ways to have it sharpened and to influence others. Now comes an extremely important chapter: body language; you will use it a lot when you are trying to persuade or manipulate another.

Chapter 9: Body Language (Analyzing, Understanding, and Reading)

Many studies have been conducted on body language, and it is the source of many myths, such as the claim that 93% of communication is non-verbal.

Although it became popular because many who read it vowed to repeat it, the actual research to begin this belief has too many inadequacies to bring to the surface. However, the impact of body language on our social skills cannot be ignored; it is also a mirror of the true emotions of our interlocutors.

Surely, you know some people who generate distrust even if they are not particularly unpleasant or mean. You don't know exactly what it is, but they give off an aura that makes you not want to confess to them your genuine emotions.

This is due to a contradiction between their verbal communication and body language. They may even have created this contradiction without knowing it.

On the other hand, others exude great charisma and are not particularly talkative. However, their physical expressions are consistent with their spoken language and convey confidence and warmth.

What Is Body Language?

Body language is a form of communication that uses gestures, signs, and body and facial movements to convey information about the emotions and thoughts of the sender.

It usually occurs at an unconscious level, so it is often an obvious indicator of a person's emotional state. Together with the tone, it is part of non-verbal communication.

Body language should not be considered an absolute truth as many environmental factors can influence it. That is why you should never conclude by looking at a single body sign. Instead, the key is to observe a consistent set of signs and rule out possible external causes (temperature, noise, fatigue, etc.)

I will show you everything you can communicate with your body and face.

Meaning of Facial Gestures

The face is a magnifying glass of emotions; it reflects the soul. But as with any non-verbal interpretation, you should be careful not to evaluate facial gestures in isolation, as they are often part of an overall emotional state and can generate multiple interpretations.

Isn't it true that when children see something they don't like, they cover their eyes and try to make it disappear from their reality? Or run to cover their mouths after lying?

Although the magnitude is much smaller in adults, we are still related to this primitive behavior in some way. This provides many clues, as many unconscious attempts to block out what we say, hear, or see can still be detected on the face.

Usually, when someone holds their hand to their face, it is the product of some negative thought, such as feelings of insecurity or distrust.

Here are some specific examples:

- **Covering or touching your mouth:** If done while talking, it could mean you are trying to hide something. If done while listening, it could signify that the person believes something is being withheld.
- **Touching your ear:** This is an unconscious gesture that you want to stop listening to words. If your interlocutor does this while talking, he probably wants you to stop talking.
- **Touching the nose:** This shows that someone is lying. When you lie, catecholamines are released, and these substances can irritate the internal tissues of the nose and cause itching. It also happens when someone is angry or upset.
- **Eye rubbing:** This is an attempt to block out what you see so you don't have to look at the face of the person being deceived. Watch out for people who often touch their noses and rub their eyes when talking to you.
- **Scratching your neck:** This is a sign of uncertainty or doubts about what you say yourself.

- **Putting a finger or something to your mouth:** It means insecurity or that you need to calm down. It is an unconscious expression of returning to the womb or the mother's security.

Head Positions

Understanding the implications of the different positions someone may take with their heads is very effective in understanding their true intentions, such as a desire to please, cooperate or be arrogant.

Pay special attention to exaggerated gestures, as they imply that the person is consciously doing this to influence you.

- **Raising your head and jutting your chin forward:** This is a sign of a clear intention to convey aggressiveness and strength.
- **Nodding:** This is an infectious gesture of submission that conveys positive emotions. It conveys interest and agreement, but it can convey that you have heard enough if done several times quickly.
- **Head tilt:** Showing your throat is a sign of submission. Doing this while nodding as you listen to others may increase the speaker's confidence in you. It has also been observed to be used to express interest in men for women.
- **Supporting the face with the hands:** The face is often exposed to "present" it to the interlocutor. Therefore, it shows attractiveness to another person.

- **Hands-on the chin:** It is a sign of evaluation if the palms are closed. If the palms are open, it could mean boredom or loss of interest.

The Gaze Also Speaks

Communication through the gaze has a lot to do with the dilation or contraction of the pupil, which responds to the internal state we experience.

This is why light eyes are usually more attractive than dark eyes: because they allow the pupils to dilate more clearly, a response associated with positive emotions.

When you speak, you typically maintain eye contact 40-60% of the time. This is because your brain is busy trying to access information (NLP assumes that, depending on the type of information it is trying to retrieve, it will be biased, but this has been scientifically proven not to be true).

In some social situations, lack of eye contact can be interpreted as nervousness or shyness, so pausing before responding can give you time to access information without looking away.

Looking directly into the eyes when making a request also helps improve persuasiveness. But the gaze has other functions.

Changing pupil size: it's impossible to control, but the presence of dilated pupils generally means you're looking at something you like, while constricted pupils are a sign of hostility.

In either case, these are very subtle changes, often overshadowed by environmental changes in light intensity. It was also discovered that mirror neurons are responsible for adjusting the size of our pupils to those of our interlocutors in an attempt to synchronize body language for greater connection.

- **Raised eyebrows:** This is a social greeting that means fearless and joyless. Do it in front of someone you like.
- **Look down:** This is considered a gesture that conveys sensuality to attract men among women. Indeed, many of the female avatars on online dating sites are taken precisely from above (sometimes with the additional intention of showing cleavage). For men, the opposite is true: low shots look taller and more dominant.
- **Gaze:** For women, making eye contact for 2 or 3 seconds and then looking down can indicate sexual interest.
- **Repeated blinking:** This is another way of trying to block the person's view in front of you, possibly out of boredom or distrust.
- **Sideways glance:** Another way of expressing boredom while unknowingly looking for an escape route.

Smiles Types

You can use this section when trying to persuade or connect with someone. You can use the smile from the list and apply it according to your intention. You can rehearse it in the mirror to bring it out as needed.

A smile is an inexhaustible source of meaning and emotion. There are many benefits of smiling and the possibilities of communicating with it. In addition, thanks to mirror neurons, smiling is a highly contagious behavior that inspires positive emotions in others.

Several types of smiles can be distinguished depending on what they convey:

- In a fake smile, the left side of the mouth tends to lift more because the part of the brain that is more focused on emotion is located in the right hemisphere and controls the left side of the body.
- A natural smile (or Duchenne smile) creates wrinkles around the eyes, raises the cheeks, and slightly lowers the eyebrows.
- A tight, silent smile indicates that the person does not want to share their emotions with you and is a clear sign of rejection.
- The biological function of a smile is to create a social bond that builds trust and removes any sense of threat. It also happens to convey obedience, which is why people who want to appear powerful and women who want to maintain authority in a typically male professional environment avoid smiling.

Arms Positions

Arms and hands together provide support for most of the movements you make. They also allow you to protect the most vulnerable areas of your body if you don't feel confident.

Proprioception tells us that the communication pathway between body and mind is mutual. For example, when you experience an emotion, your body automatically reflects it, but the opposite happens: if you voluntarily take a posture, your mind begins to experience the feeling associated with it. This is especially noticeable when you cross your arms.

Many people think they cross their arms because they feel more comfortable. But gestures are considered natural when they align with a person's attitude. However, science has shown that crossing them encourages a critical attitude no matter how comfortable the gestures may seem. Remember that you don't cross your arms when you spend quality time with your friends.

This is the message you send when you take a certain pose with your arms:

- **Crossed arms:** It indicates disagreement and rejection. Avoid doing this unless you want to send this message to another person. In sensual settings, women often do this when they find it too aggressive or unattractive in the presence of men.
- **Crossing one arm in front to hold the other:** This shows a lack of confidence because you need to feel embraced.
- **Arms crossed and thumbs up:** Defensive posture, but at the same time wanting to express pride.
- **Holding hands in front of the genitals:** For men, it provides a sense of security in vulnerable situations.

- **Hands clasped behind the back:** It shows confidence and boldness by exposing weaknesses such as the abdomen, throat, and crotch. It can be useful to take this pose in an insecure situation to try to gain confidence.

Generally speaking, crossing your arms means you are experiencing insecurities. Hence the need to protect the body. There are many variations of adjusting a watch, holding a briefcase in front of you, or holding both bags to your chest, but they all mean the same thing.

Hand Gestures

Hands and arms are among the most flexible parts of the body and therefore offer a wide range of non-verbal communication possibilities. However, they are most commonly used to denote body parts, to show authority, or sexual desire.

They also help support verbal messages and give them greater power.

A part of the brain called Broca's area is involved in speech processing. But it turns out that it can also be activated by moving both hands. This means that gestures are directly related to speech, so gesturing while expressing yourself can even improve your language skills—great for people who get blocked when speaking in public!

A study also showed that reinforcing sentences with gestures brings to mind words that will be used more quickly and make your message more persuasive and understandable. In addition, the study found that the most persuasive gestures were those that were consistent with the verbal meaning, such as pointing backward when referring to the past.

Here is all the information about the meaning of the gesture:

- **Showing your palm open:** This shows you as someone sincere and honest while closing it shows the opposite. You can use it when persuading to gain trust.
- **Hands in your pockets:** It denotes a lack of involvement in the conversation or situation.
- **Emphasizing something with your hands:** When someone makes 2 points with their hands, they usually use their dominant hand (palm up) to emphasize their favorite point.
- **Interlocked fingers:** Expressing a depressed, anxious, or negative attitude. If your interlocutor takes this posture, break it up by giving them something to hold on to.
- **Fingertips connected:** Expresses confidence and security but can be mistaken for arrogance. For example, it is very useful to detect if your opponent has a good hand when playing poker.
- **Putting the other hand behind the back:** Trying to control yourself, thus expressing frustration or trying to hide nervousness.
- **Thumbs out of pocket:** For men, this represents an attempt to show confidence and authority in the presence of the woman they are attracted to, although in conflict situations, it can also be a way of conveying aggression.

- **Stick your thumbs in your pockets only:** This pose outlines and highlights the genital area and, therefore, is a sexually open attitude in which men show no fear or sexual interest in women.
- **Putting your hands on your hips:** This indicates a subtle aggressive attitude because you want to increase your physical presence. Many men use it to create an advantage in their social circle and appear more masculine in front of the women they attract. The more the chest is exposed, the more subtle the aggression.

Legs Position

The legs play a very interesting role in body language. The farther the limbs are from the central nervous system (brain), the less control the rational mind has over them, which means greater freedom to express inner feelings.

Generally speaking, human beings are programmed to move toward what they want and away from what they don't want. The way someone places their legs can give you some of the most valuable clues about non-verbal communication, as they tell you where they want to go.

- **Forefoot:** The forefoot almost always points to where you want to go. In social situations where there are several people, it also points to the person you find most interesting or attractive. If you want someone to emotionally feel that you are paying attention, make sure your feet are in front of them. Similarly, when your interlocutor points their foot at the door instead of at you, it's a pretty obvious sign that they want to end the conversation.

- **Legs crossed:** This is a defensive and closed attitude to protect the genitals. In the context of courtship, it can convey a woman's sexual rejection of a man. In a social situation, a person sitting with legs crossed can mean that he or she is not interested in the conversation. Indeed, researchers Allen and Barbara Pease conducted an experiment that showed that people remembered fewer lecture details if they listened to a class with their arms and legs crossed. Sitting with legs crossed, in women, usually means a certain shyness and introversion
- **Sitting with one leg raised:** Typically masculine, showing a competitive attitude or willing to argue, this would be the seated version of crotch showing.
- **Legs apart:** Another masculine gesture that wants to convey dominance and territory.
- **Sitting with one leg parallel to the other:** Several authors recognize that, in women, when it comes to drawing attention to the legs, it can be interpreted as a courtship, as they are more exposed to this pressure position and provide a more youthful and sexy appearance.

Learning to detect inconsistencies between speech and body language can be very useful. The signals sent by the body are usually very reliable because humans cannot control all the signals it sends.

Remember that you have to interpret all these body signals in a global context and with certain limitations. Don't conclude with a single gesture. Someone might just sit and look a certain way because they are simply cold or because it is a sport that they have mechanized and taken away with real meaning.

I recommend that you practice the positive and open posture I describe here to increase your self-confidence.

Chapter 10: Using Body Language for Persuasion

Now that you know what body language is, as I taught you in the previous chapter, you must see the uses you can make of it in the subject we are dealing with in this book, persuasion. Here's what you can do to impact and engage.

Did you know that you can only influence others through gestures, and what your body says will make them trust and respect you, or not? I show you how to use persuasive body language to gain influence through your gestures to earn the respect of others and make people think you are someone worth listening to.

You Can Make a First Impression in Just Seconds

How long do you think it takes people to make a first impression on you? Depending on who tells you, anywhere from 7-30 seconds. The exact number doesn't matter. What is important is that it is made in a short period.

What does it mean? Your first impression has to do with what they think of you, which is why it's so crucial that you know what your body says.

You can easily gain people's respect and trust if you get it right. If you don't, they are likely to ignore you or walk away from you, which can be very damaging on a social and professional level.

What can you do to make the best first impression through your gestures? Imagine you have the most important meeting to date, someone who can change the trajectory of your life. Today is the big day, and you're feeling very excited.

You've been preparing for weeks. Finally, you're dressed to win and plan to challenge the world.

Picture this:

After you've been waiting in the room for a while, you're invited into the meeting room of the large microchip company where you are. There you are greeted by a person in an important position. You see each other, and you notice that you immediately have a crush. You walk with a firm step and the certainty that you will show the best version of yourself.

As you exchange smiles, shake hands, and say good morning to each other with total sincerity, the energy in the place leaves you with a good feeling that you will get that job you are longing for in the big multinational technology company.

Now imagine this:

As you're on your way to that interview, you find the traffic backed up, thicker than ever, drizzling, complicating everything. You left home early because you're a punctual person, but you didn't make it on time. You get to the building, and the elevator is full, so you decide to take the stairs up the 13 floors. You arrive anxious, sweaty, and almost hyperventilating. You are greeted at the reception desk and are shown in immediately.

As soon as you enter the meeting room, you exchange glances with the person waiting for you and feel a kind of coldness, almost disappointment. With your head down, your reaction is to break eye contact because you think this situation overwhelms you. Without looking at you or shaking your hand, he asks you to sit down, giving you the feeling that you got off on the wrong foot.

How do you imagine each scenario will play out? The first impression is the unconscious reaction that you generate in others at the first contact, and it will condition how they will treat you from that moment on.

Three Questions that Are Asked in that First Impression

According to Vanessa Van Edwards, researcher and founder of Human Sciences, we will decide in seconds whether we will like and trust the person or not. It is an instantaneous judgment that occurs even before the first word is uttered.

Due to evolutionary issues related to survival, our defense mechanisms lead us to make immediate decisions about whether to fight or flee, and we decide this by seeking answers to three key questions:

1   Is it an enemy or a friend?
2   Is it a winner or a loser?
3   Is it a rival or an ally?

The first point we need to know is whether we are safe or in danger. If you are a friend, there is nothing to worry about. If you are the enemy, maybe you are.

Therefore, you need to find out right away if he or she is a winner or a loser. This will help you understand the ability to carry out the intention when it comes.

If it is the "enemy" and the "winner," it is likely to attack and hurt us, in which case we will have to decide whether to flee or defend ourselves quickly. If they were a "friend" and a "winner," they would likely calm down, and we would let our guard down. We will stop following "friends" and "losers" because it brings us nothing if it is "friends."

Once it is understood that he or she is a "friend" and a "winner," the question arises whether they are potential "allies," i.e., whether they are willing to use their skills for possible cooperation.

No, we are no longer under constant surveillance in the civilized world because there is no real death threat. But the impact of first impressions still plays a role in us and helps us decide with whom to start a stronger bond.

How to Show Persuasive Body Language, Capable of Influencing People

By taking care of our first impressions and what we say with our gestures, we can regulate how other people answer these three questions about us, how they will treat us, and what we have achieved in our interactions.

I want to go one at a time.

Enemy or Friend?

If you want that person to answer in mind, the key is that you look for them to feel comfortable in your presence. When he sees you as a person with good intentions, you achieve this with transparency and positive emotional contagion.

When your intentions are opaque or appear bad because you project negative emotions, the other person feels uncomfortable and wants to find a way out.

Conversely, as former FBI kidnapping chief Chris Voss said, "when someone feels good about you, you make them smarter." This is because your subconscious mind stops worrying and lets your conscious mind focus on you.

A gesture that conveys transparency of intention is the display of hands with open palms and no objects. An open hand is an unarmed hand that does not attack. So, handshake in the West.

Avoid putting your hands in your pockets or behind your back; at least make them visible at first.

Also, we humans are emotional animals and convey our emotions to each other. If you want the other person to feel an emotion, you have to feel it and then project it through your facial expression.

When you first meet, smile, or at the very least, show a friendly gesture. This will convey friendliness and make the other person feel good.

Loser or Winner?

For this person to see you as a winner, the key is for you to project a body language of confidence, which will be interpreted as competent. For example, imagine a person who feels defeated, has just lost a competition, has received bad news, or has despair over current circumstances. What do you see?

From an evolutionary perspective, physical strength has always been associated with the ability to achieve goals. Weak body language means not being able to deliver. Strong body language is the opposite, which increases your social value.

People who show confidence are often confident in their abilities and help others be confident. You can communicate assurance and confidence through gestures with your eyes, hands, and body.

Looking away can signify insecurities, lies, or apathy. Conversely, maintaining eye contact generally shows that you believe what you say and have nothing to hide.

Crossing your arms can convey apathy, insecurity, or closure, saying between the lines that you don't want to be here. Instead, open your arms and gesture to show that you are an open and confident person.

Rival or Friend?

The key to getting the other person to respond "ally" is to make them feel important in front of you. This is the human need.

Remember a conversation where the other person seemed to be there while your thoughts were elsewhere? How do you feel? Bad.

We feel valued and important when we are listened to attentively. When it comes to interacting, it's not enough that you intend to pay attention; you have to demonstrate it physically. You will do it with your whole being, but especially with your head, torso, and feet. Use your head, and when you agree, they'll know you're listening by your assent.

Looking them in the eye and helping them appear confident promotes connection because, through eye contact, both people secrete oxytocin, the hormone of trust and emotional intimacy. Just be sure not to impose it on people with a fixed gaze and narrow vision, as it can appear hostile.

I challenge you: Ask someone you trust (a family member or friend) to do the following exercise with you. For 30 seconds, look the other person in the eyes, don't look away, don't say anything... Those physical sensations you will start to feel are oxytocin.

Using your body, you can also say that you are interested in talking. You'll do this by showing your torso as a sign of accessibility and also by leaning slightly toward each other as you listen to them. But, again, be careful not to get within a personal distance of fewer than 1.20 meters from them.

Finally, in a face-to-face conversation, your position will show your focus of interest. If you look at a person, it will reveal that you are interested in what they want to tell you.

Learn How to Influence Others With Your Body Language

- Friends, winners, allies. If you use gestures correctly, you'll get three reactions.

- That's it. Learning body language skills is great for self-assessment. Indeed, if you ask someone to videotape you during an interaction or presentation, you can find out what your body is saying. This way, you can enhance the positive aspects and improve the negative ones.

- However, I ask you not to memorize the gesture, period. Because if you do that and try to force them into your interactions, it won't feel natural and will make others suspicious.

- The real key to using gestures to influence others is to eliminate your habitual bad practices and then understand that natural gestures result from your emotional state. Therefore, if you can control your emotions, your gestures will help you influence others.

- If you care about the other person, your body will tell you so, and you will feel important.

- Your body will draw you in emotionally and feel comfortable if you feel genuine appreciation.

- If you have confidence in yourself and what you say, your body will help them trust you.

At that point, the magic of influence will pass through your gestures, and you will be the person others will want to listen to. Here are some elementary body gestures you have to do.

Always Make Eye Contact

This is basic advice. Eye contact, even for evolutionary reasons, is seen by those who hold it as a symbol of strength and security. How do you convince others without self-confidence?

Have a Firm Posture

Lift your chest, straighten your spine and open your compass slightly. In short, stand erect and firm. All this is natural, not like a stiff and severe soldier. Not fixed or rigid, but strong and confident. Whether walking or sitting, you can maintain a firm posture because it reflects your inner security. By the way, exercise helps: Work your back, shoulder, and abdominal muscles.

Smile

Emotions are extremely important, and teaching as old as Aesop's states that you attract more flies with honey than with vinegar, so smile.

Gesticulate

Spread your passion! Facial expressions, gestures, and all that your body can do are resources that can generate empathy in those who listen to you so that they believe your thoughts and accept them.

Use Your Voice and Words Properly

Speaking fluently will make others think you are knowledgeable and trustworthy. However, the famous rhetoric is not acquired for free, nor is it innate, but like other qualities, it is nurtured and tempered. Read and listen to radio shows or podcasts that feature debates and conversations. You can also imagine that you are in a situation that prohibits you from being quiet. Follow your train of thought, and you will surely have a lot to say.

Be Aware of Some Inflections

Try not to use a flat tone. Instead, turn up the volume if necessary, point it out if you ask a question, and also if you use an expression of admiration. If you want to capture your listener's attention, make your voice an unexpected way for them.

Draw on Silence Using Intelligence

As in music, silence is an element of speech that you can use to enhance your expressiveness. For example, after asking a question, a brief silence can make the other person feel drawn in and therefore included, even if you are going to answer. Silence also gives the impression of intelligence, thoughtfulness, and even a complex mind.

Use Words According to the Effect You Want to Achieve

Words have a specific weight, just like physical substances, mainly because we understand them only in terms of their relationship to each other. Some words make us feel good, some remind us of painful situations, and some can scare us or even make us angry. What impact do you want to make on your audience, and what words would you choose to achieve it?

Use Some Objects

Certain items will unknowingly impress the audience. For example, a pen used as a baton can generate the idea that, like a driver, you can control the situation. Smoking a cigarette while you speak can bring an aura of expertise to what you say. Finally, by connecting you with people engaged in learning, fidgets with glasses can bring the seriousness that has historically been attributed to these accessories.

Nod More

This very simple behavior creates an atmosphere of trust with the audience. Still, you should use it with moderation and subtlety because abusing it can make the other person believe that you are just flattering them.

Try to Stop Nervous Tics

Emotional insecurities manifest themselves in very specific ways: some people rub their ears, others touch their face, others start to move their legs in desperation, etc. Pay attention to what you do when you are nervous, and when you have tics, avoid them.

Relax, But Don't Overdo It

At some point in the convincing process, it may help to give a sense of relaxation. Spread your legs slightly, take a deep breath and smile calmly. Don't overdo it, though, because you don't seem to care what you say or who hears you.

Get Close, but Only Close Enough

Physical methods are also symbolic. When we approach someone to tell them something, there is a sense that we are revealing something the other person doesn't know, that we trust that person, but at the same time, it can be seen as a threat, a desire to impose dominance.

Make Physical Contact

Used sparingly, physical contact can cement impressions of trust and intimacy. Additionally, some gestures, such as hugging or holding hands, generate thoughts of protection, concern, or care for the other person. However, it should be noted that resorting to these depends largely on the type of relationship you have with the other person.

Get Moving

This can be a great resource to reinforce the impression that you know what you are talking about. The restlessness of the body can make you believe the restlessness of your mind. If you are going from place to place, it is because you are living your life the way you want to; it is not keeping you in one place.

Check Your Mood

There are at least two ways of behaving that almost guarantee that you will never be able to convince another person of anything. One, is the excessive rigidity, a kind of arrogance that some look down on others, nestled in their ivory columns. The other is a swamp of self-esteem, where not even the speaker believes what he is saying.

Relax

You may think that I am repeating myself here, but this is not so. In this case, it is about a relaxation that is deeper and more general. Being relaxed creates the impression of self-confidence and self-assurance.

Do Not Exaggerate

As Borges, Wilde, and other writers know, emphasis on literature has the paradoxical effect of weakening creative expression. Speak loudly and confidently, but not so loudly that you sound like a fascist leader is shouting to the crowd. Move and gesticulate, but don't go to extremes like pantomimes and clowns. Look into other people's eyes but don't let them water because you forget to blink by looking into them so much. Be persuasive, but don't make it seem like the only purpose of your life or the only thing that defines you as a person.

Be Sincere

Finally, be honest. Suffice it to say that nothing is more convincing than speaking from the heart. And, in the same vein, nothing scares us more than realizing the lies told by the people we talk to. Therefore, speak with sincerity and respect your interlocutor: you will see that they know how to thank you.

Chapter 11: The Role of Defense

You have seen the impact of body language, manipulation, and persuasion so far. I have spoken to you in some paragraphs with the intention that you use it to your advantage and in others. Also, help you identify if they try to do it with you or that you know what manipulative people do, which like everything in this world, are at a greater or lesser level. In this chapter, I want to show you the defense side: how to defend yourself if you are being manipulated, whether it is a boss, a partner, a parent, or whoever is trying to have control or already has control over you.

Although at times it may seem impossible to break that chain, if you begin to look at it closely, you will discover the rust and can easily break it and get out. The relief you feel when you break through to the other side is indescribable.

A master manipulator manages to influence your thoughts, feelings, and actions without you realizing his or her game. I will tell you how to spot this type of person.

Manipulation is the daily order of today's world. We are manipulated by power, media, and, of course, relationships. Indeed, we often encounter some master manipulators in our daily lives.

Manipulation is the form of emotional blackmail. A behavior initiated to induce another person to think, feel or act without realizing it, as the manipulator wants them to do.

That is the big problem with manipulation: it is a covert action, and its victims are not always aware of it. As a result, many take the bait and allow the manipulator to escape.

Therein lies the importance of learning to identify the tactics manipulators use. Next, I will show you how you may have been made to feel; although I have already addressed some of them from another perspective, I show them here from the victim's approach.

You Feel Guilty and Don't Know Why

A power manipulator continually resorts to victimization. Most likely, they have a "catch-all trauma," i.e., some problematic episode in their lives that they always expose as a reason for doing things the wrong way.

Phrases like "difficult childhood," "ungrateful child," and "bad luck" are their favorites. However, they found that displaying these emotional scars with some sense of pride, and even eventually bragging about them, served their purposes.

For example, if you complained about their lack of consideration, they would reply, "You're angry because I don't pay attention to details, but I had to endure my father's abandonment when I was three years old." You are disarmed in the face of their trauma. Who would be so insensitive as to make demands on someone who brought up that past? That's your game.

They Subtly Threaten You, and Sometimes You Don't Even Realize It

Indirect threats are one of the most common tactics among manipulators. From big leaders to domestic stalkers, including experienced advertisers, they use it and continue to use it. This strategy involves predicting the worst possible outcome of some of their actions.

"If you keep eating like this, in six months you'll be like a whale." They don't want you to eat, and they probably do not argue about what they say.

They just don't want you to eat. Maybe, they're annoyed at how happy you are eating ice cream, or they think you're spending too much on food. They won't publicly tell you what they think; they'll just declare a disaster.

They Use Sarcasm to Disqualify What You Do

If there's one thing manipulators hate, it's direct communication. "They don't call you a dog, but they give you a bone," goes the popular saying. They often use sarcasm to mock you or devalue your thoughts, feelings, or actions. Manipulators want others to feel insecure and inferior.

An example of this is when they send you a seemingly friendly message, but it contains quite aggressive content: "Maybe you'll have more outstanding friends if you read more. Your friends are poor devils."

The victim of a manipulator sometimes believes that these types of evaluations are the way to help them improve. Nothing could be more untrue. Use direct and honest communication when someone wants to help another person. Also, you did not disqualify them but made a specific contribution.

They Are Charming Most of the Time

The typical horse trainer knows that "the horse is petted and ridden." They usually start their work with kindness and excellence. They are enthusiastic about you and show refined taste, super fun conversation, and great "sensitivity" to your expectations.

This is the first act. In the second act, things start to change. Once they've convinced you of what a good person they are, they spring into action, accusing you of manipulating everything to show charisma.

They throw you a net of temptation, and you can't evaluate them objectively. However, you will see what they do with a good eye, and, despite the suspicion that assaults you from time to time, that person will always find a way to remind you that "you can't have a bad opinion of an amazing person."

They Claim to Be the Judge of Your Life

Somehow, the master manipulator suddenly becomes a sort of "spirit guide" for your life. They are very good at telling others how they should live, even if they don't put into practice everything they preach.

They give you advice or expose you to great philosophical aphorisms. They tell you what to do step by step. If it doesn't work, they will blame you. They tell you what to do, and it's up to you if you don't follow the instructions in the letter they so generously gave you.

A good friend, a good counselor, someone who loves you and wants you to be free and not dependent will not tell you what to do. Instead, they help you spot different solutions because we are all different, and an answer that works for "A" may not work for "B."

They Have the Ability to Speak and Also to Change the Subject

Manipulators are usually also masters of the art of speech. They use beautiful and smooth lessons. They always have some surprising or witty argument, even if it is based on a lie.

If they laugh at you and say, "You look like a penguin in that dress," and you are upset, they will immediately add, "Sorry, I didn't expect you to be so sensitive to jokes." Yes, or yes, they always win. They are silly magicians.

If you confront them, they may not respond to you. Instead, they move the conversation to other topics, and when you least understand, they're talking about things that have nothing to do with what you originally stated.

They Flip the Cake Easily

"Flipping the cake" means they break the glass, but you end up paying and making all kinds of excuses.

A very classic example of a master manipulator is a cheating husband on his wife. When the wife pulled out the motel bill she had found in his pocket, he became enraged and told her to get out and stop spying on his personal belongings. He began to talk at length about the importance of trust in relationships and respect for space.

In the end, the woman felt so bad that she ended up begging him to forgive her for being so "controlling," and the infidelity issue ended up seeming like a misunderstanding that should not have happened.

I will talk to you about this in the other section.

Manipulation in the Couple

Romantic love and misery seem destined to go hand in hand. A cliché like "who loves you makes you cry" or being a couple where you have to give in instead of finding yourself, at its core, often represents the imbalance between the two people in the couple: one manipulating, the other succumbing.

Manipulation is defined as implementing a series of strategies, attitudes, and messages aimed at achieving our goals, even at the expense of others. The most common tools used are lies or threats (often covert) such as power, persuasion, emotional blackmail, etc.

This behavior can occur in any area of life, work, family, social, much more than you think in relationships, so it is important to know and be informed to discover it. We can have a relationship with a controlling person without realizing it. But there are always warning signs, and in this combination, "pain and guilt" predominate.

These Are the Weapons They Use

The main resource to manipulate people is "emotional blackmail, which is more deeply rooted in society than we think. It takes the form of questions such as "What are you doing?" "Where are you?" and "Do you love me?" These are expressions to induce negative emotions in the other person so that they will do what the manipulator wants to do.

These are people with an interest in using various weapons or strategies.

Some of them are:

- Quarantine, which includes separating or alienating the manipulated person from their important relationship environment (family, friends, work, study, hobbies, etc.), promoting the idea that these people are inconvenient for them and establishing the marital relationship as the most important, relevant in life-space.

- Selection and control of the information received by the manipulated members in the interest of the manipulator (so-called "gaslighting"). These people use the frequency of lying and ridicule and attribute malicious traits to any information that deviates from their interests. Thus, little by little, the manipulator strips the manipulated of their critical capacity, making them doubt their reality and attributing to them the cause of the problem, such as "it's not like that," "you're imagining it," or "you're crazy."

- Manipulators apply rewards and punishments selectively. Any attitude or behavior that deviates from their interests is singled out and punished, provoking fear and guilt ("How could you do this to me," "I didn't expect you to do this," "What a disappointment"). "Good" behavior is rewarded emotionally (positive reinforcement) or calmly for not starting an argument (negative reinforcement).

- Love bombing is another tactic used by controlling people, especially at the beginning of a relationship. It involves extreme attention and intense flattery towards the other person through compliments, gifts, and details to win them over and gain their affection and trust. Once the perfect combination has been established, the manipulator begins to use other tools, such as those mentioned above, to shape their desired behavior and establish their role of authority. In this type of couple, the relationship is asymmetrical, unsatisfying, and addictive for the manipulated partner.

The repeated and prolonged use of all these manipulation strategies leads to creating a state of dependency. The manipulated person believes that they are with the one they want and that they will not find a better person than their partner is the cause of the problems in the relationship. The victims believe they need their partner to be happy.

Signs You Have to Detect So That You Run

These are situations that you have to take into account to discover that you are in front of a manipulative person:

- Change your attitude when he reminds you of his bad times. For example, "Because my ex cheated on me and I had such a bad time, I need you not to talk to that person because it reminds me of those times when I was suffering."
- When he keeps reminding you of what they have done for you.
- When you are responsible for his emotions. For example, if they are angry about something you did or said.

The person being manipulated mustn't jump to conclusions because of their insecurities that they are imagining or exaggerating something normal. To avoid this, understanding what happens during the time couples spend together is an important clue. It is normal for people to know why they decide what they do and trust their position in the short, medium, and long term. However, when a decision results from manipulation, it is less likely to reach a consensus in the medium or long term.

Another key that helps to detect manipulation is how we explain the why and what of our decision to another person. For example, if the way we are discussing our decisions is "I do what I do so my partner doesn't get mad," "I feel like I owe him," "what he did for me, I have to sacrifice too, or "poor thing, I feel bad," it may be worthwhile to assess whether there is a manipulative drive.

One of the most dramatic forms of manipulation is known, as a result of a famous classic movie, as gaslighting, to make those who experience it deny reality, feel they have a mental problem, and believe that what they see does not exist. I described that at length previously in this book. The psychological advice is to validate our emotions and perceptions, and when in doubt, compare them with someone outside the relationship to get a reference that is not manipulated.

Manipulative People Profile

Experts highlight these character traits you have to take into account:

- They are very convincing and confident people, or so they appear to be, but they are insecure and have low self-esteem deep down.
- They act for their benefit and are self-centered.
- They cannot empathize with others, whom they usually objectify and use as a means to achieve their ends.
- They usually can find the weak points of others and use them for their benefit.
- They tend to control others well and tell them what they should do. They set long-term goals.

How to Get Out of the Manipulative Situation

We can speak of different degrees of manipulation. The leader of a team of psychologists in Sikia assures us that not all blackmail is equal in intensity, and those who perpetrate it do not have the same awareness — driven by sheer ignorance. In the end, love and relationships are learned, so why not learn to love yourself?

However, in some cases, the relationship cannot be saved. Where are the limits? If your happiness, peace of mind, and emotional health are compromised, and you don't feel you have the energy or desire to fight for it, leave the relationship, and don't allow anyone to subdue your will.

Every healthy relationship is characterized by meeting the needs of both partners and placing and meeting them on an equal footing. When an asymmetry is detected, the manipulated person must begin to take responsibility for their care, claiming their limits as soon as possible.

Changing the dynamics of a relationship is not easy, and there is often a fear that "it is not going to be what you want it to be." Doing couples therapy can help guide this bonding process. Still, it is important to remember that it only works when both partners make an effort and change those dysfunctional dynamics in therapy.

Here is what you need to do when you decide to take the step to get out of this cycle:

Become Aware

The first thing is to make yourself aware that you are being manipulated. **You have rights that cannot be violated, among which are:**
- Right to be treated with respect.

- Right to show your opinions, feelings, and ideas.
- Right to set your priorities.
- Right to say no without feeling guilty.
- Right to defend yourself from external aggressions, whether emotional or physical.

If you feel that you cannot exercise these rights when you relate to others, you think you may be manipulated.

Identify Your Behavior With Other People

Manipulative people tend to act differently with different people because they have to use different relationship strategies to achieve their goals.

Take Time to Reflect

Although I have told you before that manipulative people are not impulsive in their actions, they are very anxious to know the answers to their demands. This is because they know that the longer the other person reacts, the less likely they will respond to their request with "yes."

Say "NO"

Don't be afraid to say no to their demands. We often agree to perform certain favors because we feel we owe them something, but we do not. Stand up for what you believe in and refuse to do anything you don't like or agree with.

Mark Distance

Learn to keep a safe (emotional) distance. Just like on the road, if you are near someone who might suddenly "turn or swerve" and hurt you, simply back away and keep a safe distance to avoid their strategic approach. No one can hurt you without your consent.

It's Not Your Fault

Again, you can't take responsibility for everything that happens around you, so if this starts to occur, figure out what's going on.

Be Firm in Your Decisions

Manipulative people can identify vulnerability and hesitation. If they have the slightest suspicion that your denial has the slightest chance of ending up as a yes, they will try to exploit it at any cost.

Control Your Emotions

If they see you throwing a tantrum, they will use it to their advantage because they will make you feel guilty so you can accept their demands.

Accept Their Personality

These people do not change their behavior; it is almost impossible to get them to change their ways. Therefore, I suggest that if you can't handle this type of acting out in a way that doesn't manipulate them, the best thing to do is to distance yourself from the manipulator.

Avoid Futile Conflicts

If you feel that someone is trying to manipulate you and take advantage of you, don't say anything because they will always use this behavior for their benefit.

Questions to Ask Yourself

Asking yourself a series of questions in time can save you from continuing to suffer for that person:

- Do you think what you are asking me is reasonable or at least a little fair?
- According to you, what should I answer?
- Are you asking me that, or are you just telling me?

Questions of this nature can make the manipulator think that his plans have been discovered, and, as such, he is likely to look for another victim who is more sensitive to his charisma.

You Must Take the Necessary Time

It would be best if you took the time to respond to their request. They often play under pressure to get answers right away, they don't let you think, and the pressure makes you finally give in to their demands. Just hurry to love; for the rest, take your time.

Be Firm

Be firm in your assertion. They are great experts at reading your non-verbal communication. If you falter or waver, they will notice and work harder in anticipation of your downfall.

Now you know. If you cross paths with one of these evil soul criminals and manage to recognize them, don't hesitate to turn them into a simple, vulgar, out-of-work sausage with all the weapons at your disposal right now.

Chapter 12: Deception

I think you already understand the power of dark psychology and persuasion and that if you know how to use it, you can find great purposes. At the end of the previous chapter, I talked about how you can get rid of this kind of person. Still, it is not only what they cause in your life, but it also is not that you use it for your benefit and get that customer of the technology brand, immense, which increased your company value, or that you got a job in the other company, or got a promotion; even if you used it with bad intentions and got that partner who was your competition to leave. Universal history is full of manipulated people, and thanks to this, history was written differently. That is what this chapter called Deception is about, the great manipulations of people throughout history.

History is written with blood and words. The most famous rulers of world historiography go down in history for their deeds and actions that were significant in changing the course of their empire or nation. But they are not alone. Behind them are family members, followers, and trusted people who sometimes exert an invisible force on monarchs or politicians, dragging them into the decisions that will determine their destiny. In this regard, I have unveiled some of the most famous manipulators in history who have existed and will be remembered for their contributions in the shadows.

Joseph Goebbels

German Joseph Goebbels will forever be remembered as one of the great figures of the Nazi regime. Always in the shadow of Adolf Hitler,

Goebbels exercised enormous influence over the party and government propaganda in control.

Given the importance of Nazi party propaganda and public events, Goebbels was probably the most powerful man in Germany after Hitler. Parades, marches, mobilizations, speeches by the Führer, everything in Nazi Germany passed through Goebbels' hands, which meant always bearing the relentless signature of German politicians.

He led several movements and was one of the most productive manipulators in history. For example, he exerted pressure on the population to arouse hatred of Jews, raised the people against the communist regime in the Soviet Union, or made possible various party mobilizations in his favor, such as collecting valuable materials and money to support his party.

Under his command, he was responsible for Germany's ruthless persecution of Jews due to his oratory, manipulative skills, and hatred of non-Aryans.

Olympia, the Mother of Alexander the Great

This is another great historical figure of manipulation. Olympia, the mother of Alexander the Great, has always been portrayed as a dark person with a lot of power behind the scenes. It is said that she could manipulate her son into betraying his father Philip and suggesting the expansion of the empire into Asia.

Alexander the Great has always been considered a great warrior with extraordinary fighting skills, but for many historians, his mother Olympia ruled at the political level. So much so that even after Alexander the Great's death, Olympia exercised her power in an attempt to put her grandson in charge of the kingdom of Macedonia and his entire inheritance.

Rasputin

Tsar Nicholas II will always be remembered as the last emperor of ancient Russia before the communist system came to power. For many historians of the time and 20th-century scholars, his biggest mistake was to shift power and send Rasputin, a steppe-created healer who could barely read or write, to be his penitent, indeed his only ally before his death.

It is said that Rasputin arrived in the Russian capital as nothing more than an orator preaching the word as a Messiah. However, everything changed when Rasputin prayed for several nights for the tsar's son, who became the so-called savior. The baby had hemophilia but improved under Rasputin's influence in court.

From that day in 1905, the tsar and a good part of the nobility fell at the feet of this great manipulator who dragged the Romanov monarchy to disaster.

Vizier Ay, in the Shadow of Tutankhamun

The legendary Tutankhamun went down in history as one of the most famous monarchs of ancient Egypt. The truth is that the pharaoh reigned for ten years, from the age of 9 to 19, and everything he achieved was the result of the great previous work of one of his closest official, the Vizier Ay.

The official ruled Egypt during the infancy of the future pharaoh and, with a closer look at the people, was very successful among Tutankhamun's subjects.

For many, he was also responsible for the pharaoh's death. However, the Vizier Ay did not want his power to change once the pharaoh was old enough to rule alone, so, in the absence of evidence, many believe it was Ay who killed the pharaoh.

After Tutankhamun's death, the Vizier Ay married the pharaoh's sister and took the throne.

Charles Maurice de Talleyrand-Perigord and His Manipulation of Napoleon Bonaparte

Napoleon is considered one of the smartest rulers in history, but Charles Maurice de Talleyrand was probably much more intelligent than him. The man served as the conqueror's foreign minister. He made sure Napoleon didn't sabotage anything he was doing behind his back, such as signing treaties with Austria and Russia to create a better world than the ruler could ever imagine. When Napoleon learned of his betrayal and sent other ministers to accuse him of the crime, Talleyrand responded tactfully, "It is a pity that so great a man should have behaved so badly," according to the documents. He was dismissed and at that point became the beginning of Napoleon's downfall.

Yelü Chucai Manipulated Genghis Khan

Genghis Khan is known as the greatest conqueror in history. The leader of the Mongol Empire changed the world with his fighting skills and the way he united different types of people in his rule. Behind him, in his circle of parliamentarians, Yelü Chucai was one of the most cunning and sickly people in Khan, and he managed to change things. The emperor wanted to kill everyone, burn down the city, and let his people rebuild everything, and Yelü Chucai tried to convince him that it was better to save the city and rule the people to contribute to the empire. He finally succeeded and remained by his side until his death.

A man can change his mind with a gentle whisper, which shows the fragility and innocence of human beings. Yet, too often, we deny the truth or believe in the uncertainty of our destiny and get into other people's minds or ignore that others make decisions for us. Do you have total control over your decisions? Maybe you will find an answer you don't want to see if you look back.

Chapter 13: Seduction Using Dark Psychology

Body language is behind every social interaction we have daily. Although we don't realize it, we use it in everything we do.

In this way, body language is part of non-verbal language, including body position and movement. Of course, you already know that from everything you've read here.

Through body language, you can express yourself in many ways: gestures, facial expressions, postures, eye contact, or distance from other bodies, always leaving aside words or phrases suitable for spoken language.

Sometimes body language plays in your favor, while other times it can play a trick on you, you can always use it to bring out your subtle and emotional character to attract other spontaneous aspects such as seduction and attraction in this case.

The truth is that body language, although in practice it is almost always accompanied by spoken language, can have a lot of power on its own.

Now that you know more about body language, do you know how to use it to seduce someone you like?

· How to Use Body Language in Temptation

Body language can be more important than verbal language when it comes to seducing or trying to attract a person.

This language activates neural mechanisms that have been involved in reproduction for millions of years. Thus, since our actions are spontaneous and unconscious, it isn't easy to control them and their effects on those who see us. However, it is not impossible to gain ease and fluency in controlling body language, so you can use it to model non-verbal language and arouse interest in others.

Here are several strategies you can use to help you begin to gain the confidence of others:

Maintain Eye Contact

Don't avoid the other person's line of sight. This is a crucial step because while you don't need to look them in the eye constantly, you should be aware that you need to maintain eye contact.

One trick is to point your eyes toward the top of the other person's face so that your eyes naturally turn in the right direction without having to fixate on the pupil.

Show Confidence Through Leg and Arm Position

Tension and insecurity can be seen in many poses, especially in the position of the limbs.

Confidence is reflected in the fluidity and lack of stiffness of arm and leg movements. Go back to what I narrated in the chapter on body language and use it to your advantage.

Making the Post Parallel to the Other Person

You should not only look in their direction, but it is always better to have your body facing each other.

Keep Your Hands Free

Avoid putting your hands in your pockets or crossing your arms, as this is an important part of your body that should accompany what you want to express.

Align physical proximity with the level of intimacy and comfort exhibited by the other person.

You should not assume that being too close to others or touching them too much will make them like you more, but physical proximity should be associated with comfort.

Therefore, you can be neither too close nor too far away. Keeping an appropriate distance can show interest, and it will be an opportunity for the other person to show if they feel the same way.

Don't Hold Back Smiles

Even if you don't think your smile looks good, as long as it is genuine and natural, in most cases, it will build a stronger relationship.

Therefore, this will make the other person relax and feel comfortable, so you should never suppress your smile. How can you seduce with words in this way?

Covert Orders and Squirrel Phrases

A covert order is a command or suggestion hidden in words that lead a woman to think or feel something in particular. For example, when talking about relationships, you might say, "Imagine how you feel when you contact someone, and you want that person to come back for more information." In this example, you would instruct a woman to recreate that feeling of connection in her mind.

To evoke emotions in women, you can use squirrel phrases to introduce covert commands or suggestions, phrases that allow you to sneak commands into speech. Some of these might be like "Never mind...," "You'd better not think about...," "I'm sure...," or "We shouldn't..."

Use Trance Words

Trance words have a special meaning for people and can move their emotional parts. They are very important and often repeated words for a person.

If you talk to a woman and use her trance words, you create a feeling of intimacy and comfort between the two of you. How to do it? I will give you the following examples:

She said she wanted a man who would make her feel comfortable. ("Feel good" is her trance word). Later in the conversation, you say, "Wouldn't it be great if you could be with a guy who could make you feel good, let your guard down, and feel comfortable? You know what? I have a feeling that could be happening to you right now; stay with me."

To put this topic in context, I'm going to quote one of the most interesting passages from the book *The Neil Strauss Method*, the moment when Neil meets Ross Jeffreys and uses an anchor to seduce the waitress:

"Let me ask you something: how do you know when you like someone? Or, put another way, what signal do you get from him that tells you from the heart?" At that moment, he lowered his voice and read each word extremely slowly — "does that... boy... really... attracts you... very much...?"

I later learned that the purpose of the question was to associate emotion with Ross's face, causing the waitress to experience the desire that accompanies attraction in his presence.

She was silent for a moment, thinking. "I think there's something strange in my stomach, a tickling sensation." Ross put his hands to his stomach, palms up.

"I understand," he said. "And I guess the more attracted you are to him, the more ticklish you get." He slowly raised his hands to his heart. "They'll hold you until you blush, like now."

That's what anchoring is all about, she whispered; it's about attaching a physical emotion like a sexual desire to a gesture. Now every time Ross raises his hand like he just did, she will feel the attraction to him.

It only took a while for the waitress to start to cloud over; she would raise and lower her hand like an elevator, from her stomach to her heart; she smiled as she watched her blush constantly.

"Were you immediately attracted to your boyfriend?" Ross asked her while snapping his fingers to snap her out of her trance, "Or did it take a while for that desire to appear?"

"Well, it took a while," she said. "Yes, it was a little late in coming. In the beginning, we were just friends."

"Don't you think it's better to feel the desire from the first moment?" She raised her hand again, and the waitress's gaze clouded again. Then Ross pointed to himself in what would be another strategy and led her to think that he was the man who made her feel that desire. "Before you go, I want to propose the following: Why don't you take those good feelings you're having right now and put them in this sachet of sugar?" He took an envelope of sugar and rubbed it against his raised hand. "So, it will go with you all day long."

He offered her the envelope with sugar. She put it in the apron and left, red as a tomato.

"What you have just seen is an example of spicy anchoring," said Ross. Even when he is gone, the sugar sachet will allow the waitress to relive the emotions she has experienced with him.

For me, this is one of the most enlightening passages and contains more than I read in that book. It speaks so much that it takes several readings to break down what is going on in this single scene.

The first thing is that the subject of this excerpt is anchoring, a process so simple and powerful that we use it without knowing it, and some people don't because they have no idea how useful and effective it is in sex. Let's define anchoring from one side, gradually approaching its core and then its application.

When we evoke a particular experience, we relive all the sensory information captured and stored at that moment. For example, when you think of a vacation at the sea, you begin to think of the smell of the beach, the sun's warmth, the coolness of the beach, and the bright sun that you cannot look directly at. Perhaps, you too relive the feeling of the joy of swimming, and you may even hear the voices and conversations of those you are traveling with. Another example would be when you are with someone special, maybe on the radio or at the disco, and a very special song plays; after a while, when you listen to that song, you start thinking of that person, maybe it is a good feeling, maybe you feel it now when you read me.

This means that any specific sensory information can serve as an anchor for a memorable experience (i.e., a song, a movie, a sunset, a sound). It is also possible to construct an external stimulus and intentionally link it to an experience, to relive it when desired. This becomes the anchor point in its most theoretical definition, as in psychology, which is called modulation of reflexes by stimulation, a system studied by the Russian researcher Pavlov.

Through this process, valid experiences can be mobilized to be used successfully in specific situations, such as experiences of falling in love, creativity, security, etc., and even negative experiences can be mobilized or awakened to be associated with someone or something, such as competition or competitors.

Anchors can be visual (gestures, imitations, photographs), auditory (intonation, speed of speech, volume), and kinesthetic (tactile stimuli), but there are also olfactory and gustatory anchors.

In the book *The Method*, Ross uses three types of anchors:

1   **Visual:** Moves the palm at the stomach level.

2   **Auditory:** Changes the speed of the voice, for example, when he says: "Or, in other words, what signal is coming out of there, from inside, telling you... every word is extremely slow—that... boy... really...attracts...you...a lot?" He also uses snapshots.

3   **Kinesthetic:** He delivers the sugar envelope, which makes her, whenever she comes in contact with the envelope or touches it, she feels that. Even the sugar envelope theme is a symbol and an interesting strategy.

The kinesthetic procedure is the simplest and most widely used: it consists of associating a person's specific experience (difficult or pleasant situation) with tactile stimuli. Kinesthetic anchors can be established in various body parts, such as knees, hands, shoulders, arms, fingers, etc. It is important to note that the person applying the anchor always adapts the pressure of the contact to the intensity of the response shown by their interlocutor, increasing or decreasing it according to the changing response of the anchored person.

For example, suppose you want to associate a pleasurable experience (such as a vacation) with yourself. In that case, you must be attentive to recognize when the other person is at the most reactive level, i.e., when they are happier, more joyful or more in love, more confident, or more creative. You will see it in the color of their skin, in their face, in their smile, in their expression.

There are several places in the text where we see Ross anchored at the height of the reaction. For example, when the waitress blushes, when she talks about the tickle in her stomach, or when she laughs. He also managed to link the memory of the emotion of falling in love with the movement of her hands, which produced a distinct physiological response in the waitress: blushing.

In our context, it's not very easy to anchor by touching a person. However, in the clip, we also see that Ross doesn't touch her, the reason being that you can't touch strangers. So, the best way to do it is with his actions (as Ross does when he moves his hands up and down his stomach.) It is a visual stimulus; he also uses auditory anchors by modulating his voice.

And I wonder, how many of you are so addicted to the sound of your phone that you jump out of your seat just listening to it? Here's an everyday example of an auditory anchor.

Or have you ever seen those letters on a BMW? They are a symbol, just like Apple, which has an apple, KFC, which has a Colonel, and McDonald's, which has an evil clown. Well, the idea is that you associate a visual stimulus (a symbol, a gesture) with an experience, like the comfort and luxury of a BMW, or the taste of KFC chicken or a McDonald's hamburger.

Anchoring techniques are often associated with themes known as "peak moments," when someone's life situation is particularly emotional, such as being happy, feeling absolutely content, or falling madly in love. What Ross does is awaken this peak time with a question:

"How do you know when you like a person a lot?" This is a simple question, but one that leads people to review how they felt when they liked someone internally. She then began to remember the sensations in her body (especially in her stomach), and it was at that moment that Ross took the opportunity to create his visual anchor (the movement of his hands).

With that action, he has connected with her mind. However, you must also remember that he is also beginning to adjust his voice, putting her in a very small trance. In this way, Ross makes sure that she understands his words completely and is not distracted, and she can get a deep experience and answers, rather than simply saying, "I don't have time for stupid questions."

This is all very interesting, to tell you the truth. Once you connect the emotional experience or peak moment, with the memory of the attraction symptoms, you start making suggestions.

"I understand, and I guess the more you're attracted, the more flirtatious you're going to feel — slowly move your hand up until it reaches the level of your heart — they'll go up until you're blushing like you are right now."

And begin to secure the anchor, move the hand steadily until you secure control of the association with the emotion that is Ross's attraction.

Also, in the end, Ross associates the feeling with the face when he points to himself when he does the routine of asking her for the image of the person she felt attracted to. In addition, the care he takes in this quote is noticeable:

"Don't you think it's better to feel that desire from the first moment?" She raises her hand again, and the waitress's gaze becomes cloudy again.

No doubt it's the same sequence; it's the anchor and the suggestion. He tells her that it is better that she feels that from the first moment and frees the mind from that obstacle that prevents her from feeling the desire in the first moment, which makes her an easy woman, then anchors that feeling of desire and remembers that it was a lot of tickling in the stomach with the anchor.

Let's say that schematically it would be something like:

- Arouse the experience on an emotional level in an intense way through a question.
- Wait for the peak time, when the person physically tells you that they are coming to relive the experience. If you ask him or her about a pleasant experience, they will change their expression, laugh, or change their gaze; if you ask about a painful experience, they will lower their eyes, close their lips, etc. Wait.
- Now, anchoring an unpleasant experience is useful when you want to break a habit like smoking or overeating.
- You can anchor as you like.
- Verify with the other person, evoking and revisiting the experience repeatedly in conversation. Notice how Ross is a great conversationalist and asks many questions/statements and tips on the same topic.

You can make suggestions that strengthen the link between the emotion and the anchor you have decided to use.

Use Reverse Psychology

Reverse psychology works even for women who are less likely to pay attention to you and is a subtle way to influence their motivation.

The founder of logotherapy, Austrian neurologist and psychiatrist Viktor Frankl, used reverse psychology extensively. While it has some degree of manipulation or influence over a person's behavior, it is very effective in generating attraction and can therefore be used to subdue the other.

In the realm of emotion, reverse psychology involves masking an interest with an opposing attitude to generate a desire for proximity. It is important to note that this technique does not always work because there has to be a previous resort.

It works when the person has stopped calling or searching and just wants to have a relationship without commitment. Emotional intelligence needs to use these techniques very carefully to be successful and get close to that person.

You have to know that to get a woman's interest, you have to stop calling and texting her repeatedly; avoid this behavior for good.

Make her feel that you are not there; give her time to think about you. She will get bored of you if you are always over that person, and she will think about you if you are not there.

When she suggests a plan, you should not show that you are available and accept it right away. Instead, mention what you will be busy with, tell her about your plan, and, if it is obvious that you do not need her there, be very witty to not appear arrogant or overbearing. She is not friendly, you want to go with her, but you cannot.

You should not make things easy for her. Only then, she will wonder what motivates you and make interesting assumptions about you.

When you are with that woman, it shows that you are a complete person, you don't need anyone's love to feel complete, you enjoy life, you are happy, you are not in a hurry to find love, give her time, don't think of her as your only option, you have so many possibilities, you shouldn't just set your eyes on her.

If you go out with her and she tells you or hints that you will be nice as a friend, respond that you think it's a good idea and feel happy about it.

It is great if you tell her that she is a beautiful woman who is a good match for someone like that; she will feel that you are not interested in her.

In this way, the desire to have something will grow more and more. Remember that people always want things that are hard to get or things that others desire.

Chapter 14: Is Manipulation the Same as Persuasion?

Many people do not know the difference between persuasion and manipulation; they think that the two concepts are the same or very similar.

I present to you the analysis of the differences between those concepts by our founder Angel Taboada Novelo for his book *Persuasion: The Power of Leaders*:

"The difference lies in the means used and the intention to achieve one versus the other. Persuasion is when you prepare a person to accept an alternative point of view or voluntarily change the original course of action for your benefit and that of others. Manipulation is when you force a person to change the course of action to benefit only yourself."

These are the main characteristics of each:

Persuasion

- It is when you respect other people's feelings and beliefs.
- Motivates the other person's needs and desires to be met.
- Look for a win-win situation for everyone.
- It provides the information necessary for the other person to decide that best suits their interests.
- It raises what the other party has to lose and what the other party has to gain.
- It establishes communication with the mind and heart of the other party.

- The results are effective and with more permanence, because it achieves conviction.

Manipulation

- It is characterized by overriding the beliefs and feelings of the other person.
- It forces the other party to comply with their wishes.
- The result is a win-lose situation, the one who manipulates wins and the other loses, or else both lose.
- The manipulator uses any means to force the other person to do something for their benefit.
- The manipulators put forward what is best for themselves at that moment.
- Manipulators request or complain to get what they want without taking into account the wishes of the other person, i.e., they practice blackmail.
- The results only last until the real motives they are scheming appear.

You may be asking yourself, what does the manipulator want to do? Why do they work so hard to manipulate others instead of focusing on improving themselves? The truth is that manipulators have a deep psychological need to control others, so they try to "weaken" their victims to dominate them. When they manipulate others, they try to overwhelm their willpower, destroy their self-esteem, seek passive-aggressive revenge against them, or obfuscate their reality and make them more malleable.

Manipulators Aim to Reduce Your Willpower

Willpower diminishes. Thanks to our willpower, we can maintain control over our lives and resist people's attempts to dominate us and force us to obey them. This is why one of the main intentions of manipulators is to destroy our willpower.

How can someone take away your willpower? First of all, you must understand that willpower is not infinite. We can lose willpower through a process that psychologists call "losing the self." To understand this, you have to think of willpower as a renewable resource, but slowly. If we spend those resources on one thing, we can spend less on other situations that require it. Therefore, ego depletion is the result that happens when we use all our willpower, and don't have enough to face future challenges.

Controlling people know that willpower does not come from a bottomless well, so they tend to overwhelm us when we are forced to deplete our willpower. For example, a malicious person may keep trying to make you angry when trying to remain calm. However, if he continues to do this over a prolonged period, he may reach the point of angry outbursts and reactions.

Psychologists believe that willpower is like a muscle: it gets stronger when you exercise but fails when you don't use it. Malicious people will counteract your willpower by forcing you to work too hard. Willpower allows us to make the right decisions in the face of temptation or stress. This makes us spend time studying for exams instead of watching videos online. Without willpower, we are vulnerable to people's signals to do what they want with us.

Self-exhaustion is sometimes referred to as "decision fatigue." The idea behind this concept is that the more decisions we make, the more tired we become, and, as a result, we are unable to make good decisions. When controllers put us in situations where we have to make constant decisions, they end up exhausting us. Several other factors are known to weaken willpower. The first is scarcity; when something is in short supply, we become more impulsive to acquire it, abandoning our principles in the process. For example, when a person is hungry, he or she may be forced to leave the principle of "no stealing" to stay alive.

Those who have the capacity for emotional manipulation can reduce the other's willpower by introducing feelings of lack. For example, when a person shuts you up, they essentially withhold interpersonal interactions and feelings, which creates a feeling of scarcity for you. This increases the likelihood that you will leave the position and comply with their request. Another way to deprive someone of willpower is to threaten their happiness or livelihood. Malicious people will damage your willpower by doing things that jeopardize your job, relationships, or happiness. Your willpower is most vulnerable when a co-worker does something that threatens your job security or your partner does something that ruins your life. Commitment makes you give up or do something against you.

Stress is another factor that can lead to willpower burnout. When we are constantly stressed, our mind fills with worries, clouds our judgment, and we end up making bad decisions. Malicious people work overtly and covertly to introduce stressors into our lives in the hope that the resulting stress will drain all our energy and make us more susceptible to manipulation. When manipulators succeed in taking our willpower, they gain the power to control us and tell us what to do; we will begin to delay judging them and lose our identity.

Manipulators Destroy Your Self-Esteem

In addition to draining your willpower, malicious people want to destroy your self-esteem. Unfortunately, there are many different ways to do this. Despite our attempts to strengthen our self-esteem from within, the truth is that as social beings, we place a lot of value on what others say about us, and therein lies the power to control others. Manipulators can lower your self-esteem by using well-crafted phrases to attack or undermine. Their words are often intended to anger or confuse you, as you will spend a lot of time thinking about what they mean. We have discussed the types of manipulation techniques that can cause you to begin to question or emotionally weaken yourself.

Manipulators will also constantly blame you for various problems and diminish your self-esteem. When someone keeps telling you that something is your fault, the seeds of doubt begin to grow in you, and as that thinking deepens, you begin to internalize the other person's criticism, which can ruin your life or your self-esteem; a controlling person can blame you without even saying a word. When bad things happen, they will look at you and tell you everything you need to know about your feelings, and even without accusations, you will begin to question yourself.

Another way manipulators destroy your self-esteem is by inundating you with negative information. We all know that our self-esteem can be affected by our relationships with others. If we are surrounded by negative people who keep badmouthing us, we begin to internalize these attitudes. Manipulative people, especially Machiavellians, can trick us by giving us negative information. For example, a co-worker might keep throwing cold water on all your ideas until you start to believe you can't do the job. In relationships, manipulators can destroy your self-esteem by emotionally ignoring you until you begin to think you don't deserve to be loved and to love.

Controlling people can also destroy your self-esteem by satisfying your fears. Once they discover that you have certain fears, they will begin to recreate them to use against you. The more fear we have, the lower our self-esteem. Manipulators love it when the victim feels inferior for various reasons. You've probably heard the saying that if you don't support any beliefs, you end up believing anything. That's what the handler is counting on here. They know, and if you don't have a solid vision of who you are, they can gain the power to control how you see yourself. If you start questioning your identity, they take it upon themselves to create a version that they can handle.

Manipulators also know that we can be likable when we have low self-esteem because we want to please others to get positive attention and gain their approval. They want their victims to be likable and want to put themselves at the center of their victims' lives to benefit from them. At work, manipulators may want to destroy your self-esteem and make you feel you are not up to the job so they can crush you and get to the top. If they can't completely convince you that you are a loser, they will be content to make you so afraid of failure that you can't even muster the courage to compete with them.

Manipulators may also want to destroy your self-esteem so that you can't maintain personal boundaries, and they can come in and take advantage of you. As we mentioned, when self-esteem is destroyed, the person is unable to stand up for their beliefs and therefore unable to enforce their principles. You may feel that you don't even have the basic right to express your preferences, so the robotic arm can move freely around you.

Manipulators Seek Passive-Aggressive Revenge

Some manipulators will pursue you as they seek passive-aggressive retaliation against you. For example, if you ever belittled a narcissist, sadist, or psychopath in any way, they may hold a grudge and manipulate you with a desire for revenge. Of course, normal people will hold grudges or persecute each other for clear reasons to both parties. However, people with dark personality traits can attack you for almost any reason, as long as it makes sense to them. There is no logical threshold you must meet to be attacked. They may hold a grudge for years for something you said. You may become their target because your boss praises you instead of them. They may even target you because of deep psychological issues they can't understand.

For example, a psychopath might try to hurt you and destroy your life because you look like someone who rejected him when he or she was a teenager. The point is that you don't have to do anything specific for the malicious person to decide to retaliate against you passive-aggressively. Unfortunately, you may remind them that they grew up with a bad parent or, in the case of the Machiavellian, you may be the one to stop them, and they may have to destroy you to move on. It could also be that they think you are weak and therefore an easy target for them.

When someone seeks passive-aggressive revenge against you, they will want to humiliate you to make you feel inferior. They think you have a good thing going, so they want to reduce it little by little, making you feel insecure. If you outperform them at work, they will want your performance to go down because it will make them feel better. These people will treat you with a lot of disguised verbal hostility. When you're not around, they spread negative gossip about you. They will take the trouble to find fault with what you do and often criticize you. They will go out of their way to minimize your thoughts, feelings, and contributions because they simply don't want you to be happy.

Some passive-aggressive people will seek revenge on you because they are miserable and love to make others unhappy too. Most dark people can't stand to see you happy when they are sad. Narcissists believe that the world revolves around them. If they are miserable, they will expect others to be miserable and try to punish anyone who is not through psychological manipulation. A sadist will be happy to make you miserable. Machiavellians, on the other hand, will plan to steal your happiness.

Passive-aggressive revenge seekers often use hostile humor in disguise to demean others. They use sarcasm to mask hostility toward others. They will say hurtful things and then claim they are "kidding." They attack people based on their physical appearance, socio-cultural background, gender and sexual orientation, level of education, and anything else they can think of. In other words, these manipulators have deep-seated issues that lead to psychological barriers and will do anything to harm others to satisfy their own psychological needs.

Manipulators also want to obfuscate your reality to have control over you. They want to alter your perception of reality because it is the best way to control and dominate you. This is because when you can convince a person that what they see and hear is not true, then you can tell them what to think, feel and value. The reality of controlling others is the ultimate dream of any manipulator. They want you to replace your perception with theirs, and when you question your reality, the chances of that happening multiply. This is why mind control manipulation techniques, such as Brainwashing and Gaslighting, are the most dangerous.

Chapter 15: Using Body Language for Persuasion and Mind Control

Body language is something very powerful that, if you know how to use it correctly, will come in handy. In this chapter, I will teach you many body language techniques to manipulate and achieve mind control.

Reject Someone with Your Body Language to Leave Them Out of the Group

If there are four people, move them away so that you turn your back on them or one of the other members turns their back on you so that you immediately leave them out of the group.

Turn Your Back on Someone to De-Emphasize

It is similar to the previous one, but you cannot do it in conversations with, for example, three people.

If three people are talking, when someone speaks, turn your back, look away, or start talking to someone else, this way you take away the importance; when you turn your back to someone, they think you are rejecting them, and if they see that, the others will also look down on them. You can do it subtly and elegantly, as long as you don't look rude when you do it.

Redirect Your Body Language to Another Side

When a person does not interest you, bores you, or you want to diminish their importance, when talking to that person, direct your body language to another side. In this way, you are taking away importance; you are telling them that you are not interested in what they are telling you, but in a polite way that they do not understand consciously, but their unconscious does. This, like the previous point, should be subtle. When you want to end a conversation, or when you don't want someone to talk to you, simply deflect your body language.

Smile

When you want a person to like you, try this test: walk into a bar and say, "Hi, can I have a latte?" Although, at first, if you're not used to smiling, you'll feel a little silly. Get used to smiling, especially when you go to bars, restaurants or meet new people. Just the act of smiling makes someone smile back or see you as more friendly and forces them to like you.

Deep Gaze to Influence Others

When someone is talking to you, and you want them to keep talking, or you want them to like you and connect with you, your gaze should be intense but not uncomfortable. This denotes that you are paying a lot of attention to that person, and they will notice it, generate more connection with you, and get along better than if you look away or talk and don't look at them. You should look deep, but not intimidating.

Body Positioning for Rapprochement

If you want to build up more power or make yourself more interesting, you can pull back with your body language, which will make the person turn more towards you and give the impression that they want to win you over. That person sees it and becomes a little self-convinced. Of course, this doesn't work miracles, but if someone doesn't like you at all, they won't turn around; on the other hand, if someone talks to you, they will be interested, or you can provoke them to notice you. Then when he or she talks to you, you back off. After that, you will see how the person keeps going forward.

Another variation is to speak in a low tone to force the person to come closer and thus generate more proximity. If you do this, do it gradually, speak normally, then lower, to force the person to come closer to talk to you.

Sit Up Straight

Leaning on a chair, resting your elbows on a table, and covering your face with your hands are acts of disrespect. They say you are not interested in what you are listening to.

Conversely, if you sit up straight with your shoulders back, you will look more confident. This is the power position. The more space your body takes up, the more successful you will be. Also, never lean back; it will make you look smaller and less energetic.

Use Gestures Correctly

If you exaggerate your gestures, people will think you are lying or trying to hide something. On the other hand, open gestures like open arms show that you have nothing to hide.

Don't Touch Your Hair

If you are one of those people who often touch, play with or try to fix your hair while talking to others, then you should stop this bad body language habit.

This indicates mental insecurity and inability to concentrate. Stop touching your hair and try to focus on what the other person is saying to you.

Spread Your Arms

When you cross your arms, you're sending a clear signal, "I'm inflexible and don't agree with what you're saying." Crossing your arms and legs is not a good body language strategy, even if you are smiling.

Keep Consistency Between Your Words and Expressions

Inconsistency between your words and your facial expressions makes it look like something is wrong. They may suspect that you are trying to deceive them with your body language, even if they don't know exactly why or how.

For example, a nervous smile when rejecting an offer in a negotiation will not help you get what you want, and it will only make the other person uncomfortable working with you.

Each of these strategies along with your body language will help you get what you want, better communicate what you are thinking, and align what you say with what you do.

Shake Hands Firmly

Never shake hands by waving them or being too soft, barely squeezing the other person's hand. When someone invites you to shake their hand, make sure it is firm. This strategy of using body language can increase trust and confidence.

The strength with which you shake hands is crucial for you to make an impact on the other person. Or, if you do it partially, it is an action that shows you have no interest in the person you are shaking hands with.

Putting your hands behind your back has a couple of meanings. Walking with your palms with your hands behind your back is characterized as someone who is reserved, shy, and prefers to go unnoticed. When someone sweats excessively in front of another person, it means that they have something that compromises them and makes them anxious.

If you are hiding your hands in your pocket or behind your arms or torso unconsciously, it is a sign of anxiety. Likewise, hands tend to have fewer regular movements than usual, so you have to pay attention to all those gestures.

Keep away from the person who is too close to you and causes discomfort without realizing it. The best thing is that when you are standing still, move one foot forward, whatever it is, to the same height, as if you were going to take a step. This way, they will know that this is their limit and should not exceed it.

How you Can Move When You Meet a Potential Customer

When meeting a potential customer, the goal is to build trust with them as quickly as possible. **Here are a few tricks you can follow:**

- Imitate that person's behavior. Don't exaggerate, but keep this in mind. If the other person moves a little while talking, move too. If they speak fast, try to speak at the same pace yourself.
- Have open body language. Relax your shoulders, open your chest, and avoid crossing your arms or hunching your back.
- Don't back away when the other person speaks; that can make you uninterested in them.
- Be close, but don't overdo it.

How to Present Yourself to an Audience

When presenting to an audience, your goal should be to coordinate your body language and your words so that the ideas you express have a more significant impact on them. **There are three specific techniques:**

1   On the key points that you want to emphasize; you need to stay close to the audience and not the presentation.

2   Don't look at the screen or computer so much. It is best to use these resources naturally and not make them the communication's protagonists.

3   Focus on your audience. I know you may be a little nervous about technical or content issues, but your audience is the most important element. Look people in the eye and make them feel you are talking to each one of them.

Body Tricks to Encourage a Shy Teammate

When you lead a team or are part of one, but you care about people on the team expressing themselves, your goal with shy people is to make them feel confident. First, notice if there is someone on your team who you think is especially shy. Is there anyone who encourages them to express themselves? Then jot down these three specific tips:

1   Align your body with them, go with the movements and generate rapport.

2   When they speak, nod your head, so they feel the support.

3   Smile and be positive while you speak, but don't do it effusively, or you will make them nervous.

Non-Verbal Communication to Become a Group Leader

When you are in front of a new team, the goal is to convey authority without being aggressive or overbearing. **Here are a few tricks you can use to do that:**

- Keep your head up and confident.
- Relax your shoulders and keep them back.
- Don't slouch; keep your trunk straight.
- Lean forward a little when you speak to convey certainty and involvement.
- Lean back a little when you want others to speak.

What to Do When Socializing With a Client

When socializing with clients, as in a business coffee, your goal is to keep the contact purely professional: polite but approachable at the same time.

Here are six specific tips:

1. You must be attentive and listen; you have to focus on what the customer is saying.
2. Have eye contact to convey total commitment.
3. Smile and nod frequently.
4. Never flirt. Although you may make a quick sale with some specific customers, you will generally convey a poor professional impression.

5   Don't groom yourself in front of the customer: no hair, suit, or general grooming, and don't clean your teeth with a toothpick.

6   Don't interrupt. Keep in mind what the client has to say; their message is more important. Find areas of common interest to take a moment away from professional topics to generate empathy and connect.

Strategies to Show Disagreement Without Making Enemies

Disagreeing with what someone thinks in a professional context is tricky because it can damage their self-esteem and even disappoint them.

When you want to disagree, the goal is to signal what you think but to generate an alliance with the other person instead of fighting.

Here are some tips to achieve this:

- Smile and nod your head when the other person speaks and convey receptivity.
- Make physical contact with the other person in an appropriate and non-threatening way.
- Show your palms when you show your opinion and be less threatening.

Body Language in a Job Interview

When you go to an interview, your goal is to build confidence and trustworthiness as quickly as possible. **To achieve this, here are three specific tips:**

1 You can lean slightly toward the interviewer when you speak and stand up straight when he or she is speaking.

2 Use the relationship skills learned in this book to mirror your physical demeanor.

3 Keep your body language open, relax your shoulders and move your hands so as not to convey a defensive or fearful attitude.

How to Deal With an Upset Colleague

When dealing with angry colleagues, your goal is to show them that you understand how they feel. Your impulse may be to enter their circle of anger, but that doesn't help anyone, so try these three specific tips:

1 When the other person speaks, keep your arms outstretched but not close to your body; you will convey a sense of security.

2 In the same position, lower your palms. This calms the opponent's subconscious.

3 Listen and reflect on his or her emotions, though not at their level. For example, if he or she tells you how angry they are via their facial expressions, shouting, and raised arms, you need to only convey a little of the same facial expression with your face. In this way, you will communicate to them that you understand how they feel by listening to their reasons.

Body Language for Asking for a Promotion

When approaching your boss for a promotion, your goal should be to maintain consistent body language so that his or her brain is more likely to engage.

Here are four specific tips:

1   First, match your body language to his or her body language to establish mental synchronicity. Then, modify your body language to the language you want to use to achieve your goals.

2   Whether you are sitting or standing, you must remain upright. Avoid any stressful movements of your feet, hands, and fingers.

3   Your gestures should be very subtle. Don't make large, sustained movements, as they could undermine your authority in this particular situation where someone else is assessing whether you can assume greater responsibility.

4   Focus 100% on your boss. If you hear a noise in the office next door, don't get distracted by looking at documents on their desk or turning your head.

Conclusion

Let's remember a little of what I talked about in this book.

Psychological manipulation is defined as the exercise of negative influence through mental distortion and emotional exploitation to seize power, control it and use it for our benefit by affecting the victim.

In our highly competitive and often self-centered society, manipulation is a common phenomenon for both the manipulator and the victim.

Negative manipulation is designed to gain an advantage by making the victim feel inferior, inappropriate, unsafe, and under suspicion. The manipulator makes persistent and critical negative judgments, publicly scolds, humiliates, or tramples, uses hostile humor, is sarcastic, delivers unpleasant surprises, applies peer pressure, social exclusion, coldness, threats to personal safety, and privacy-related extortion.

Let us also remember positive manipulation, which is used to bribe others to obtain favors, sacrifices, or emotional commitments. This is, for example, when the manipulator provides compliments that are not sincere, appealing to vanity and false professional, romantic or social acceptance, always with a trap. They employ false professional closeness, offering help, rewards, or support with the plan to charge in disproportionate reciprocity. They also promise safety and protection after the victim has been taken without their knowledge.

Deceiving or planning to distort the victim's perception to control them more easily are among the most common types of manipulation. An example of this is lying, blaming the victim for feeling bad, distorting the truth, issuing mixed messages to keep the victim off balance, spreading them strategically, withholding privileged information, exaggerating things, exaggerating circumstances, and making a one-sided bias of the problem.

In these cases, they exploit the person's goodwill, guilty conscience, and sense of power, with the obligation to generate an instinct of protection.

Typically, manipulators pretend to be weak people, such as a martyr or helpless and defenseless human beings. They use sad stories to gain sympathy, favors, or support, dramatizing the difficulties to achieve preferential treatment based on guilt.

Another technique is the use of abuse or hostility, dominating and controlling the victim through explicit aggression. Examples include temper tantrums, coercion, intimidation, physical, emotional, mental, sexual, financial abuse, brainwashing, and oppressive restraints.

Many chronic manipulators end up paying a high price and suffering personal and/or professional setbacks throughout their lives. **Long-term negative consequences of manipulation can include the following:**

- They present multiple communication problems in emotional relationships due to their reluctance to be sincere and responsible.
- They distance themselves personally or professionally from others because they feel cheated, coerced, or sabotaged.
- They suffer damage to their personal and/or professional reputation due to a lack of trust and authenticity.
- They lose valuable job opportunities due to a lack of credibility. In the worst cases, job performance evaluations can lead to career setbacks and demotions.
- They lose moral integrity, which leads to associated insecurities and low self-esteem, as those around them know that they are "a fraud."
- It triggers self-centered tendencies that prevent a truly healthy relationship.

- They trigger passive-aggressive tendencies due to their inability to establish a truly collaborative relationship.
- They develop narcissistic tendencies due to their inability to establish true loving relationships.
- In general, relationships are more distant, draining, and stressful. As a result, manipulators tend to have many relationships.
- Manipulators may experience physical, mental, emotional, or spiritual pain due to self-consciousness (guilt) and shame.
- They may feel stressed and anxious about having to hide for fear of being found out and exposed constantly.

What Makes Us Manipulable?

In some cases, excessive empathy and, in others, fear affect our lives. Sometimes the lack of personality or calm reflection prevents us from being aware of the underlying manipulation and limiting it.

Often, the root of the problem is low self-esteem. People with an inferiority complex compare themselves with others. As a result, they think that they do not have the same capabilities or that their needs are less important. Because of this, they tend to believe that their desires are almost irrelevant and may even feel selfish when they try to prioritize them. All this makes people with low self-esteem easily prey to emotional blackmail.

Which People Are More Likely to Be Manipulative?

Well, as an antithesis to the previous paragraph, some people unconditionally recognize, defend, and prioritize their needs but underestimate or minimize the needs and desires of others. This combination makes them potential manipulators, often emotional blackmail artists.

Note that in both cases, the problem stems from the same violation of personal boundaries, but people with low self-esteem will have no or very weak limits and will be absorbed by the overwhelming needs of others; the manipulator will try to absorb and condition others in their way.

If we are aware and convinced that we are victims of manipulation, the first thing we must do is to distance ourselves from the manipulator who makes us more and more dependent. I must say at this point that it is common for the manipulated person to try to change the manipulator, but this objective is complicated. However, emotional self-defense has a motto: don't let them hurt you.

To do this, you must face the situation and ask yourself what will happen if you disobey the manipulator's demands and his emotional blackmail: Will he stop talking to you? Will he abandon you? Will he try to exclude you from the group? Will he put you out of a job?

Then, you must immediately ask yourself: Are you interested in maintaining some kind of relationship with manipulators based on compromises and power games? Are you afraid of the possibility of losing or weakening that relationship? Why? What is the source of your fear?

Emotional self-defense involves increasing our resources so as not to fall prey to blackmail or manipulation. For example, suppose you are afraid of living alone. In that case, you should list the situations in which you think you cannot live without a partner (at home, in friendship, fun...), and design an action plan with practical and concrete measures, as well as ways to overcome these circumstances, and therefore achieve independence, which in turn will make you more immune to emotional blackmail and the risk of being manipulated.

Manipulation and emotional blackmail are more frequent in people's lives than you think.

Finally, don't forget body language; I recommend learning all you can about it.

As humans, we can communicate constantly and can express our thoughts and feelings without saying a word. This is very important because body language is a form of communication and reflects who we are. It shows the ability to match the gestures of the body with the mind. For example, when you communicate your thoughts through words, the body expresses your joy or discomfort.

Human beings have a constant need to communicate because, even if they do not utter any words, they say something to others through their physical presence, their appearance, their facial features, the way they dress, their posture... Moreover, body language has more impact on the receiver than still words because images have a lot of power, and by looking, one person takes in a lot of information from another in a visual twist.

Body language shows a person's gestural skills; don't forget that the face is very expressive because expressions and smiles have a lot of power. Take control of your physical communication to help you become aware of the messages you are conveying in everyday situations, such as job interviews, first love dates, couple discussions, and more.

If what you are expressing through your body contradicts what you are expressing with words, you are sending a confusing message to the recipient. For example, if a person goes to an interview looking sloppy and late despite having an excellent resume, they are expressing a lack of interest in that job. Therefore, attention to detail is vital for better communication.

Can the manipulator improve? Maybe. But only if he or she is willing to go through a process of self-discovery. For the conscious manipulator, there is a unique opportunity to move toward the best, which means gaining a keen sense of self, acting with dignity, practicing thoughtful communication, being able to solve problems constructively, and engaging in healthy and positive relationships.

Printed in Great Britain
by Amazon